Lost Stories and Family Secrets

THE FIRST MILLENSONS IN AMERICA

Michael L. Millenson

Lost Stories and Family Secrets: The First Millensons in America

ISBN 978-0-578-93734-2

LCCN 2021912780

Cover image courtesy of the Jewish Museum of Maryland

Book design by Alissa Millenson

Lost Stories and Family Secrets

THE FIRST MILLENSONS IN AMERICA

DEDICATION

To my father, Roy H. Millenson (z"l), whose avid interest in family history inspired this book.

"We ask the leaf, 'Are you complete in yourself?
And the leaf answers, 'No, my life is in the branches.'
We ask the branch, and the branch answers,
'No, my life is in the root.'"

— The Rev. Harry Emerson Fosdick

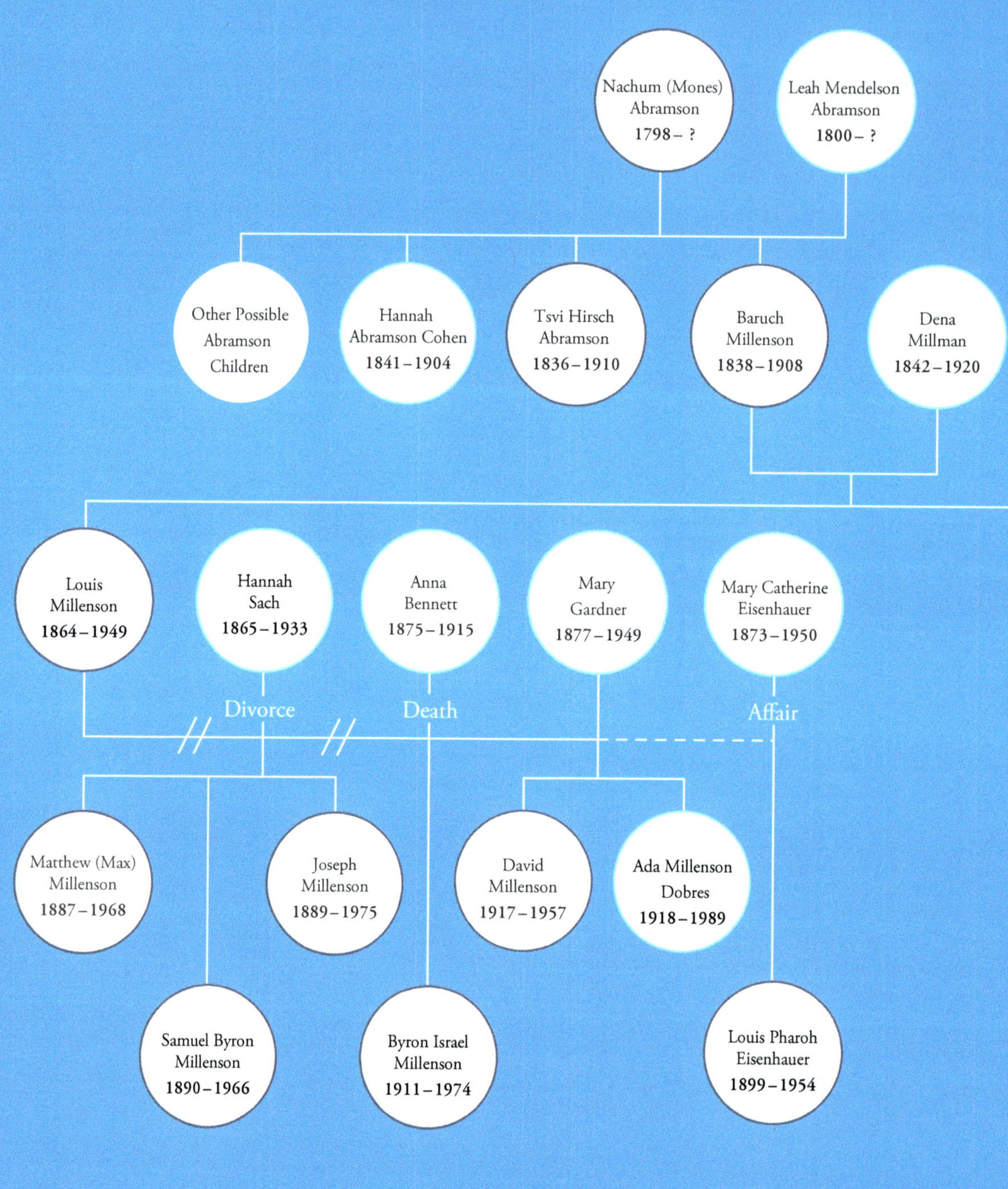

Nachum (Mones) Abramson 1798 – ?
Leah Mendelson Abramson 1800 – ?
Other Possible Abramson Children
Hannah Abramson Cohen 1841 – 1904
Tsvi Hirsch Abramson 1836 – 1910
Baruch Millenson 1838 – 1908
Dena Millman 1842 – 1920
Louis Millenson 1864 – 1949
Hannah Sach 1865 – 1933
Anna Bennett 1875 – 1915
Mary Gardner 1877 – 1949
Mary Catherine Eisenhauer 1873 – 1950
Divorce
Death
Affair
Matthew (Max) Millenson 1887 – 1968
Joseph Millenson 1889 – 1975
David Millenson 1917 – 1957
Ada Millenson Dobres 1918 – 1989
Samuel Byron Millenson 1890 – 1966
Byron Israel Millenson 1911 – 1974
Louis Pharoh Eisenhauer 1899 – 1954

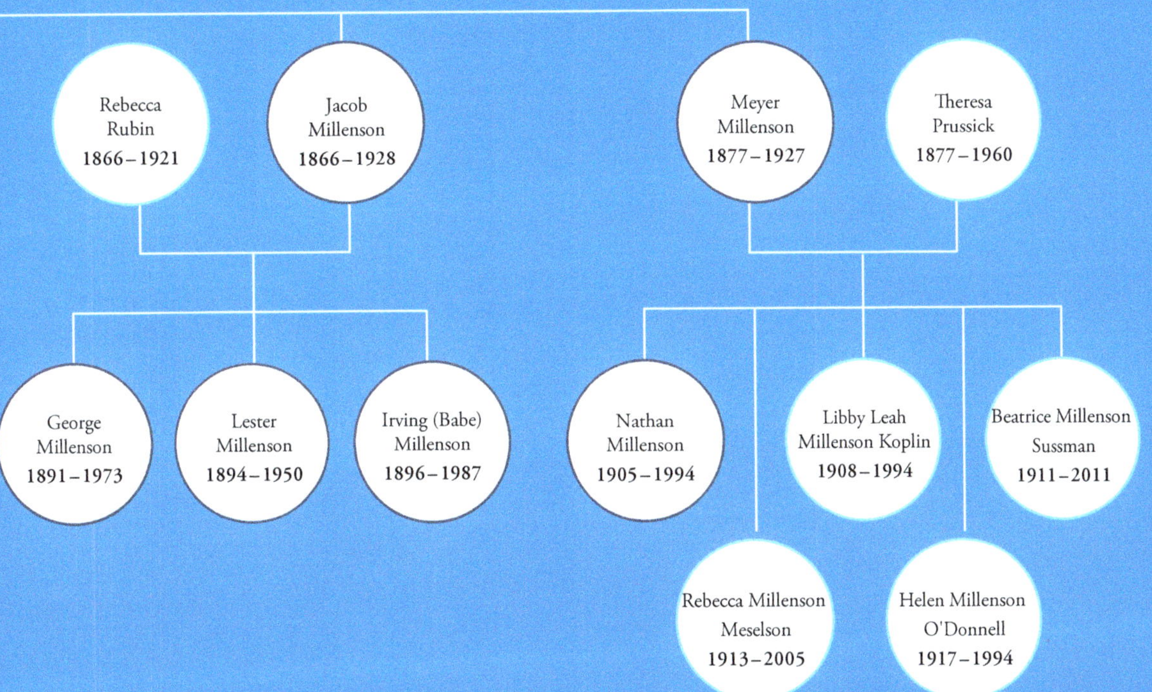
Rebecca
Rubin
1866–1921
Jacob
Millenson
1866–1928
Meyer
Millenson
1877–1927
Theresa
Prussick
1877–1960
George
Millenson
1891–1973
Lester
Millenson
1894–1950
Irving (Babe)
Millenson
1896–1987
Nathan
Millenson
1905–1994
Libby Leah
Millenson Koplin
1908–1994
Beatrice Millenson
Sussman
1911–2011
Rebecca Millenson
Meselson
1913–2005
Helen Millenson
O'Donnell
1917–1994

CONTENTS

INTRODUCTION

In the mid-19th century, a family in the tiny Lithuanian shtetl of Grinkishok changed the last name of one of its young male children in an attempt to fool czarist officials into believing the boy was an only son. It was a common ploy by the Jews of that time to avoid service in an army that drafted Jewish males as young as 12 and then kept them for as long as 25 years.

When Baruch Abramson—now Baruch Millenson—grew up, married, and had sons of his own, he went a large step further and fled from Lithuania with his entire family. This book tells the story of how the first Millensons found their way *to* America and then found their way *in* America. It covers a roughly 100-year period from the time of the name change to when the last of Baruch's three sons died.

Some of this story is inspirational, a classic tale of entrepreneurial immigrants who arrived with neither money nor language skills and slowly built a better life. They were surprisingly mobile and determinedly resilient, seeking opportunity in bustling cities and tiny towns in the East, West, Midwest, and South. One of the first American Millensons lived at some point in time in Baltimore, Cumberland, and East New Market, Maryland; Harrisburg and Philadelphia, Pennsylvania; Eastville, Virginia; Washington, D.C.; Chicago, Illinois; Milwaukee, Wisconsin; and Denver, Colorado. And that doesn't count possible family peregrinations between leaving Grinkishok and boarding a ship to America.

Some parts of this story remain deeply disturbing, even decades later. There are abandoned children, a child born of a hushed-up affair, suspicious store fires, a suicide, and an abortion gone wrong. If, as George Orwell wrote, "Autobiography is only to be trusted when it reveals something disgraceful," then this autobiography of our family is trustworthy indeed.

And some parts of this story are just plain puzzling, either because of factual gaps or facts that don't seem to fit; e.g., why Baruch's boys, products of Eastern Europe, often self-identified as German. A question that does seem to have been resolved, however, is the foundational mystery of how the Abramsons of Grinkishok came to choose the name "Millenson."

We have almost no firsthand information from the First Millensons themselves and only a handful of recollections from those who either knew them or were told stories by those who did. That information has proven invaluable, but it is fragmentary. The lost stories and family secrets that follow have largely been assembled from bits and pieces of (sometimes contradictory) information gleaned from newspaper articles, city directories, census information, court records, and other documents. There's also a dollop of DNA analysis. In addition, putting all that information into the economic and social context of the times allows us to at least make some plausible inferences.

What has emerged from this process for the first time is a nuanced picture of our ancestors as not just a list of names but as individuals with complex and compelling life stories of their own.

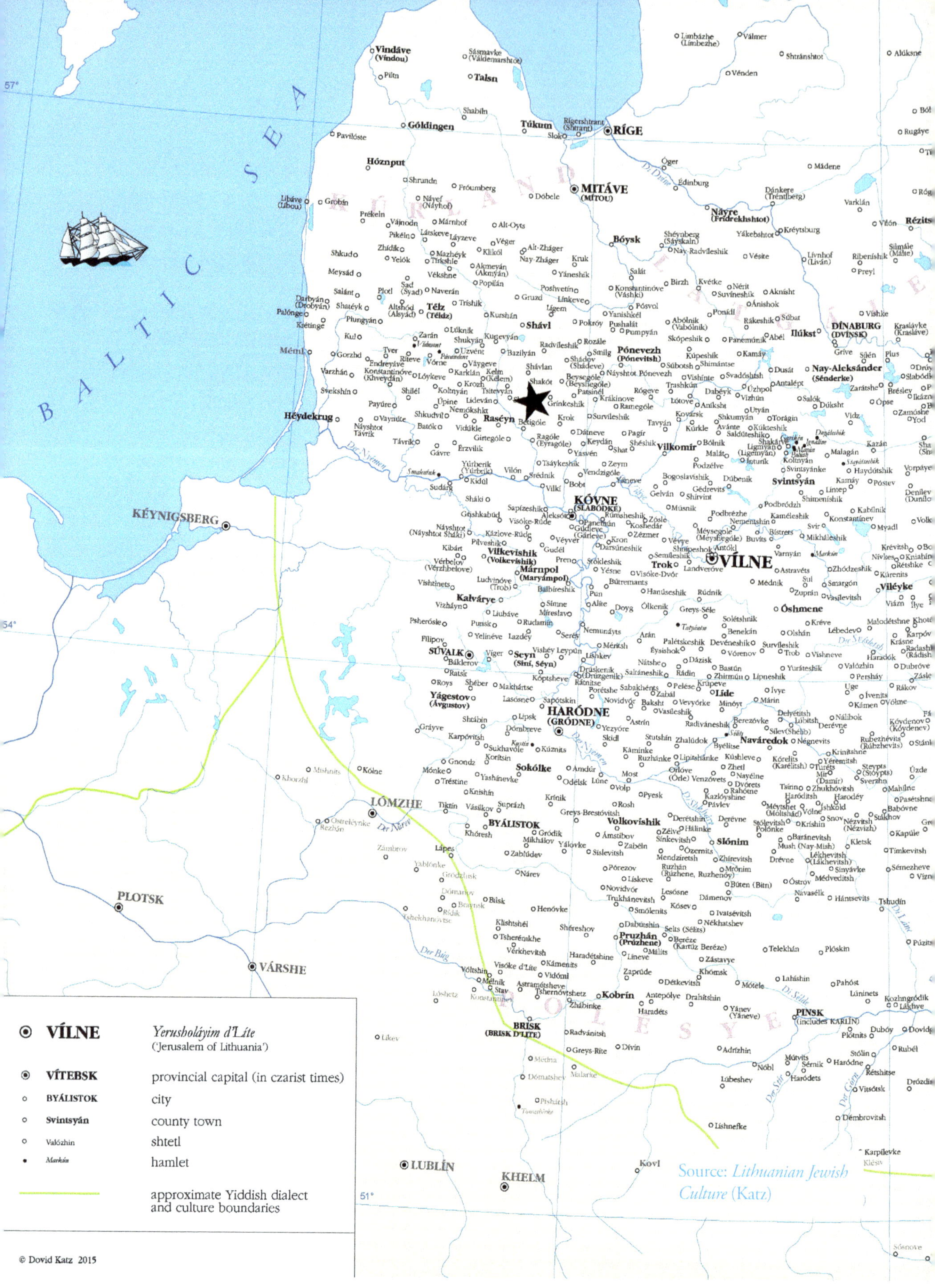

BALTIC SEA
KÚRLAND
LATGÁLE
POLESYE
57°
54°
51°
VÍLNE
KÓVNE (SLABÓDKE)
HARÓDNE (GRÓDNE)
RÍGE
MITÁVE (MITOU)
KÉYNIGSBERG
LÓMZHE
BYÁLISTOK
SÚVALK
PLOTSK
VÁRSHE
LUBLÍN
KHELM
BRISK (BRISK D'LITE)
PINSK (includes KARLÍN)
DÍNABURG (DVÍNSK)
Shávl
Pónevezh (Pónevitsh)
Vilkomír
Svintsyán
Óshmene
Lide
Naváredok
Slónim
Volkovíshik
Kobrín
Pruzhán (Prúzhene)
Sokólke
Seyn (Sini, Séyn)
Yágestov (Ávgustov)
Kalváryre
Márnpol (Maryámpol)
Vilkevíshik (Volkevíshik)
Trok
Raséyn
Télz (Téldz)
Shkud
Hóznput
Góldingen
Vindáve (Víndou)
Talsn
Túkum
Héydekrug
Mémel
Libáve (Líbou)
Nay-Aleksánder (Sénderke)
Ilúkst
Nâyre (Fridrekhshtot)
Bóysk
Viléyke
Der Nyémen
Di Dvíne
Der Nárev
Der Bug
Di Sélde
Der Stir
Der Górin
Di Láne
Di Shtshare
Di Svísletsh
Di Víliye

VÍLNE — Yerusholáyim d'Líte ('Jerusalem of Lithuania')
VÍTEBSK — provincial capital (in czarist times)
BYÁLISTOK — city
Svintsyán — county town
Valózhin — shtetl
Markún — hamlet
approximate Yiddish dialect and culture boundaries

Source: *Lithuanian Jewish Culture* (Katz)

PART ONE

Lithuania

Grinkishok

CHAPTER ONE

The Jewish presence in Lithuania, known in Yiddish as "Lita," stretches back more than a thousand years, although a specific Lithuanian Jewish identity began to arise around the 15th century. The Lithuanian village of Grinkiškis, located on the banks of the Šušvė River in the province of Kovno in central Lithuania, traces its origins back to a nobleman's estate first mentioned in the 16th century.

IN THE SHTETL

Contrary to popular perception, the shtetls where Jews lived were not ghettos. Rather, writes American scholar Dovid Katz, a shtetl was a small, "multicultural society," generally, "a town square with a church," located on flatland and "very often on the banks of rivers, streams and lakes."[1]

That description fit Grinkishok, the Yiddish name (sometimes pronounced, "Grinkichik") for what in Lithuanian was the village of Grinkiškis.

The town's centerpiece was a church that the nobleman built; however, Jews lived in the town beginning in the 17th century.[2] By the late 1880s there were about 600 Jews living in Grinkishok, or somewhere between a quarter and half of the population.

1. Katz, Dovid. *Lithuanian Jewish Culture*. Lithuania: Baltos Lankos, 2004

2. "Grinkiškis – Encyclopedia of Jewish Communities in Lithuania." In: Levin, Dov and Adam Teller. *Pinkas Hakehillot – Lita*. Yad Vashem, 1996. Accessed at: https://www.jewishgen.org/ Yizkor/pinkas_lita/lit_00197.html

In Jewish geography terms, Grinkishok sat near the far northwest border of the Pale of Settlement, which today includes parts of Lithuania, Poland, Ukraine, and the Crimea. The Pale was "the Jewish part of Russia," writes Katz; i.e., the only place in the vast Russian territories where Jews were allowed to live. Understandably, many immigrants later described their country of origin as simply "Russia."

The Lithuanian capital of Vilnius, called Vilna in Yiddish, was a major city. At one time home to 250,000 Jews, its spiritual and intellectual renown led to it being nicknamed "the Jerusalem of Lithuania." Vilna remains famous for the writings of the 18th-century Gaon (Sage) of Vilna, the prototypical "Litvak" rationalist scholar. Vilna also gave the world artists such as violinist Jascha Heifetz, painter Chaim Soutine, and sculptor Jacques Lipschitz.

Grinkishok wasn't like that.

Baruch Abramson, son of Nachum (Mones) Abramson and (we believe) Leah Mendelson Abramson, was born in Grinkishok around 1838, according to Baruch's death certificate. (His immigration record says 1836 and his 1900 Census form, 1840.) The only sibling we can identify with certainty is an older brother, Tsvi Hirsch Abramson. Recent DNA evidence, however, suggests there was also a younger sister, Hannah.

One of Tsvi's daughters, Sarah, married a neighbor named Nathan Niselovich. They changed the family's last name to "Feinberg" upon coming to America, just in case the czar's army was still searching for Nathan. Abraham Feinberg, the son of Sarah and Nathan, became a prominent Reform rabbi. In his autobiography, *Storm the Gates of Jericho*,[3] Abe related what he was told about the Old Country:

3. Feinberg, Abraham L. *Storm the Gates of Jericho*. New York: Marzani, 1965

> Not only were my parents born in Grinkishok, but their parents before them, for many generations, back to the 17th century, when a pair of ancestors fled from the Chmelnitzki massacres in Poland (of 1648). And their forebears had fled from a medieval German mob.

Grinkishok, Feinberg wrote, was a village of "thatched houses, terrible snowstorms that buried people alive and big fur hats." He continued:

> The mudholes, the box-like wooden dwelling places, the saline scent of herring, the *bes midrash* [House of Study] where males pored over the Bible commentaries and Talmud, the Friday afternoon bustle of baking and mikvah, the susurrus of prayers in the shul, the desperate hope for freedom in golden-streeted America—I knew it all from the kitchen-table talk of my parents and an occasional *lantsmann* who strayed in with precious greetings.

It was also a place where Jews were afraid to go into the street on Christian holidays and sometimes other times for fear of being beaten and robbed, wrote Feinberg. One Easter a Jewish house burned down because the Jews were afraid to disturb the Christians in church by ringing the fire bell.

Meanwhile, the Russian government itself was becoming increasingly hostile. In 1844, when Baruch was a small boy, Jewish self-governance in Lithuania was rescinded by Czar Nicholas I (1825-1855). Under both Nicholas and his successor, Alexander II (1855-1881), the Jews faced increasingly severe demands to provide young men for the Russian Army. Writes Katz:

> Jewish boys as young as twelve were taken for 25 years of service . . . . The obligation to make up numbers fell on the organized Jewish communities of each locale, and the result was the rise of the hated *khapfer* (literally, "catchers") who would in effect kidnap children to provide the quota.

Those children became known as "cantonists," a term derived from the barracks into which they were put. Many died of abuse and starvation. Jewish households attempting to evade the draft faced a fine of 300 rubles at a time when the average daily wage was less than 25 rubles, and entire Jewish communities were penalized for failure to meet draft quotas. In the province of Kovno, where Grinkishok is located, the fines in 1888 amounted to an astronomical 470,000 rubles, some of which was collected by taking over Jewish property.[4]

AN "ABRAMSON" BECOMES "MILLENSON"

It was in this context that the parents of a young Baruch Abramson—we don't know his exact age—changed his last name to Millenson so as to present him to the authorities as an only son exempt from the draft.[5] Since this was a common practice, my guess is that an accompanying bribe may have helped suppress official curiosity about a shtetl curiously brimming with only sons. Other draft evasion tactics included sending a son to live with a family that only had daughters—with the boy taking their last name—or sending a young boy away to relatives elsewhere.

To be more precise, Baruch's surname for secular purposes became "Milenzahn," as it was written and pronounced in Yiddish. In America this mutated into "Milensohn" and then "Millenson." While the name's origins have long been a family mystery, my correspondence with Dovid Katz strongly suggests it was based on the Lithuanian nickname of Baruch's mother, Leah.

4. Levitats, Isaac. *The Jewish Community in Russia*, 1772-1844. Jerusalem: Posner and Sons, 1981

5. My father's mother's maiden name was Handen. Their family's story is that three boys were placed with Jewish families that had only daughters, taking their names: Beneman, Goldberg and Handen.

The equivalent of "Leah" in Lithuanian was Ludmila, which was often shortened to Lida or Mila. Son of Mila then becomes, in Yiddish, "Milenzahn." (See Appendix A: The Meaning of the Name "Millenson.")

In 1862, Baruch married Dena Millman (as her maiden name was spelled in America) when Dena was perhaps 20 years old. Dena gave birth to Louis ("Yitzchak Leib") in December 1864 and another son, Jacob, in July 1866.[6]

The Abramson men, including Baruch, were Levites. In traditional Judaism, men are recognized as descendants of one of three groups mentioned in the Torah: *Kohanim* (Kohens), the highest priestly class; *Levi'im* (Levites), the priestly assistants to the *Kohanim*; and everyone else, *Yisraelim* (Israelites). The Torah sets forth obligations and privileges for the two priestly classes that continue to be recognized today in Jewish law in some rituals and restrictions.[7]

Baruch was a shochet (kosher slaughterer), serving Grinkishok and the small town of Baisogala four miles to the northeast. But it couldn't have been an easy living in Grinkishok, a desperately poor place. A Jewish Grinkishok resident described the conditions in 1883: "It is two years now that our bes midrash has neither candles nor wood, and the gabaim (beadles) spend their time looking for money, and all in vain."[8]

Although Baruch avoided the army, he knew his sons might not be as fortunate. Years later, Nathan Feinberg would show a mutilated finger to his son, Abe, and describe how in Grinkishok he'd stuck a knife into his trigger finger to avoid the army.

6. Dena's father's name is listed on her death certificate as Harris Millman; it is clearly Americanized.

7. A small number of Jews are *Kohanim*, a somewhat larger number are *Levi'im*, and everyone else is *Yisraelim*—plain old Israelites. This status is only passed on to male descendants. In recent years, Kohen status has been found to be confirmable by DNA testing. Levite status cannot be confirmed that way, but the marriage certificate of one of Meyer's daughters confirms the tradition that the family was Levites.

8. op. cit., "Grinkiškis – Encyclopedia of Jewish Communities in Lithuania"

We have only one piece of documentation of the family's presence in Lithuania. A list of contributors to the Persian famine relief fund, published in the Hebrew-language newspaper *Hamagid* in 1872, lists "Tzvi Hirsh ben Nachum, son-in-law of the rabbi," among an astonishing 67 donors from tiny Grinkiškis.[9] Separately, Tsvi Abramson was himself described by Feinberg as a rabbi, which in the context of the shtetl, presumably denoted some respected level of Jewish learning.[10]

Baruch and Dena had a third son, Meyer, born on April 4, 1877. Immigration records show he was born in Europe, not Maryland (despite accounts to the contrary) and in 1877, not 1876 (also despite contrary accounts). In the 1900 Census, Baruch and Dena reported having had six children but having had just three who survived. This may explain why there was a two-year gap between Louis and Jacob, which was then followed by another decade before the birth of Meyer.

My father, Roy Millenson, one of Louis's grandsons, liked to indicate someplace was in the middle of nowhere by saying it was "in *kovne gebanya*." As noted above, Kovno (in Yiddish, Kovne) was a province (*gubernya* or *gubernia*), and Grinkishok was one of its villages. As kids we had no idea that he was referring to a real place, much less a place about which there might have been family stories that could have been shared.

9. I examined the *Hamagid* list of names from Grinkiškis, and Baruch was not there. There was a Nachum ben Yosef and a Kalman ben Nachum (shown as a "boy"), but it's impossible to know if the Nachum was Baruch's father and Kalman a sibling.

10. Tsvi's listing in the Baltimore directory becomes "Abrahamson" and eventually includes the title of "Reverend."

№ 1256 1256

Verzeichniss

der Personen, welche zur Auswanderung nach Amerika via Glasgow durch Unterzeichnete engagirt sind und mit dem Dampfschiffe Prague Capitain [illegible] unter Englischer Flagge zunächst nach Leith befördert werden.

Abgang des Schiffes, d. 16 August 1881. 4th Morgens

Zuname.	Vorname.	Geschlecht männlich	Geschlecht weiblich	Alter.	Bisheriger Wohnort.	Im Staate oder in der Provinz.	Bisheriger Stand oder Beruf.	Ziel der Auswanderung, Ort und Land	Zahl der Personen	Davon sind Erwachsene und Kinder über 10 Jahre	Kinder unter 10 Jahre	Kinder unter 1 Jahr
1.	2.	3.		4.	5.	6.	7.	8.	9.	10.	11.	12.
Rurode	Ernst C.	1	—	44	[illegible]	Amerika	Kaufmann	New York	1	1	—	—
Kowatsch	Franz	1	—	29	Pesth	Ungarn	Maler	Philadelphia	1	1	—	—
Pfeifing	Jacob	1	—	22	Eschwege	Hessen	Arbeiter	New York	1	1	—	—
Backmann	Otto	1	—	28	Hamburg		Maler	Philadelphia	1	1	—	—
Wesenberg	Wilhelm	1	—	37	Stelling	Holstein	[illegible]	Chicago	1	1		
Rabinowitz	Baer	1	—	20	Wilna	Russland	Handelsmann	New York	1	1	—	—
Kränkel	Paul	1	—	18	[illegible]	Sachsen	Zimmermann	[illegible]	1	1	—	—
"	Karl	1	—	14	"	"	Weber	"	1	1	—	—
Elias	Moses	1	—	33	Kowno	Russland	Arbeiter	New York	1	1	—	—
Hasse	Gustaf	1	—	32	Berlin		Sattler	"	1	1	—	—
Fried	Baer Leib	1	—	30	[illegible]	Polen	Handelsmann	Baltimore	1	1	—	—
Mendelowitz	Isaak Jacob	1	—	19	"	"	"	"	1	1	—	—
Lipschitz	Juda Leib	1	—	18	"	"	"	"	1	1		
"	Jechiel Leibowitz	1	—	19	"	"	"	"	1	1		—
Milensohn	Baruch	1	—	45	"	"	"	New York	1	1		
Stein	Gerson	1	—	14	Warschau	"	"	"	1	1	—	—
Grünfeld	Emanuel	1	—	42	Ujheli	Ungarn	Schmied	"	1	1	—	—
Rabinowitz	[illegible]	1	—	19	Wilna	Russland	Tapezier	"	1	1	—	—
		18	—	—					18	18		

Ich erkläre hiedurch an Eides Statt, dass die vorstehenden Angaben nach meinem besten Wissen richtig sind, dass

Image: A page from the manifest of the *Prague*. "Baruch Milensohn" is the fourth name from the bottom.

Source: Ancestry.com

Coming to America

CHAPTER TWO

One of the big unanswered questions in the Millenson story is how and why Baruch and his family came to America. In the absence of solid information, we might imagine a scene vaguely resembling *Fiddler on the Roof*, with families fleeing the Cossacks on their way to Ellis Island and a life of freedom. In reality, it wasn't like that.

GRADUAL MIGRATION

The Russian Pale covered hundreds of thousands of square miles, so the situation of the Jews in Kovno wasn't necessarily the same as that of the Jews in Kiev. For example, while there was certainly persistent anti-Semitism in Lithuania, there were no Cossacks galloping through Grinkishok. Lithuania at the time Baruch left was actually experiencing relatively low levels of anti-Semitic violence.[11] Shared resentment of Russian imperial rule even led some Jews and Lithuanians to see themselves as allies.

Grinding poverty was the most powerful motivation to emigrate for Jews and non-Jews alike. There was also considerable political instability in the mid- and late 19th century as the forces of Lithuanian nationalism, Polish economic domination, and Russian repression repeatedly clashed.[12] Added to all of that was famine.

The horrors of the Great Lithuanian Famine of 1867–1869 are now largely forgotten. By one estimate, more than 300,000 people died of hunger and typhus by 1869 after two successive Lithuanian crop failures.[13] Among those who fled, many Jews went to nearby East Prussia or Poland.

11. Figures showing a growth in Grinkishok's Jewish population in the 1890s, academic monographs, and what I've seen from the stories of four or five other descendants of Grinkishokers suggests that anti-Semitism didn't ramp up to more intense levels until after the first decade of the 20th century.

12. Balkelis, Tomas. "Opening Gates to the West: Lithuanian and Jewish Migrations from the Lithuanian Provinces, 1867-1914." *Ethnicity Studies/Etniskumo Studijos* 1 (2010). Accessed at: http://www.ces.lt/wp-content/uploads/2012/03/EtSt_Balkelis_2010.pdf

13. Baker, Mark. "The Voice of The Deserted Jewish Woman, 1867-1870." *Jewish Social Studies* 2.1 (1995):98-123. Accessed at: https://www.jstor.org/stable/4467462?seq=1

Famine and avoiding the czar's draft are likely the main reasons Baruch and family left Grinkishok and, the evidence suggests, lived elsewhere in Europe before coming to America. "People quite often ended up moving gradually farther to the West," an expert on Jewish relief networks in Eastern Europe told me. "They ended up in towns where the majority of their neighbors had immigrated to previously."[14]

Certainly, famine would have had a particularly harsh impact on a kosher butcher dependent upon farmers selling him animals to be slaughtered and customers being able to afford meat. Moreover, the combined effects of famine and disease might also explain why three children of Baruch and Dena did not survive—another reason to leave.

14. Milena Zeidler, Faculty of History, Oxford University. Personal communication. February 5, 2020. Zeidler is a researcher on transnational Jewish relief networks in Eastern Europe, 1850s to 1870s.

The Millenson history my siblings and I heard growing up said that Baruch and family came to America around 1876. Documents, though, tell a different story. A Hamburg Line manifest found on Ancestry.com shows Baruch Milensohn, age 45, leaving Hamburg on the steamship *Prague* on August 16, 1881, bound for Leith, before continuing on to America.

The manifest says Baruch arrived in New York in October 1881. (Ellis Island wouldn't open for another dozen years.) Baruch's occupation is listed as "tradesman" and his residence as Sadowe, in the Polish empire, suggesting he'd left Grinkishok and lived elsewhere. Other Jews on the ship were continuing on to Baltimore, so perhaps his destination was inaccurately recorded. We have no indication he ever lived in New York, and his death certificate says he lived in Baltimore beginning in 1881. Baruch's brother, Tsvi Hirsch, who also lived in Baltimore, also lists 1881 as his own immigration year.

Meanwhile, a manifest from the steamship *Australia*, a converted cargo ship from the Edward Carr Line that crammed passengers into steerage, shows that Dena and the couple's three sons left Hamburg bound for New York on June 18, 1882. That suggests it took eight months of Baruch working and living on his own in America before he could save enough money to enable his family to join him. We have no information on where or how Dena and the children lived on their own during that time.

The *Australia* manifest lists "Dina Milson," age 40, from "Russialand" and her three sons: Leib, Jankel ("Yankel" is Yiddish for "Jacob") and "Mayer." The ages of Louis and Jacob are each about 10 years younger than they should be, although Mayer is accurately listed as age 5. The two older boys were short, and their ages may have been deliberately misstated to get a lower children's fare. Since Meyer's son will later remember his dad saying he was born in Germany, this suggests that an 1877 birth date in Maryland was deliberately contrived to make Meyer American-born, a useful fiction analogous to the fiction of being an only son that protected Baruch from the czar's draft.

THE VOYAGE

While we don't know the specifics of the Millenson family's travels, we do have a description of a similar journey from Lithuania to America. In 2009, journalist Howard Wolinsky described on a Jewish genealogical website what he learned after hiring a genealogist to trace his family's roots. By happenstance, Howard is an old friend who wrote for the *Chicago Sun-Times* when I did the same for the *Chicago Tribune*. In 1892, Howard's paternal grandfather traveled from Kovno to Hamburg, where he took a ship to Hull (in England) and then overseas to America.[15]

15. Wolinsky, Howard. "Retracing My Grandfather's Journey: Kovno to Hamburg, Through Hull to America." Avotaynu Online. December 1, 2009. Accessed at: http:// bit.ly/2Tu8hjf

According to the genealogist, Wolinsky's grandfather would likely have taken a horse cart from his shtetl to the train station in a larger town, then caught a train towards Berlin and then another train to Hamburg. The journey would have taken up to four days in a series of train compartments that were locked for the passengers' own safety, with eight people crammed together in uncomfortable seats and limited luggage space. Some people had tickets and passports, but at that time you didn't need a passport to emigrate.

The North Sea was a rough place, and the voyage was long and unpleasant. Tsvi Abramson and family spent 27 days in steerage, according to Abe Feinberg's memoir. Food, sanitation, and light were all bad.

As for Baruch's journey, the *Edinburgh Evening News* reported in its July 11, 1881, edition about an inbound voyage in which the "screw-steamer (ship) *Prague* sailed for Hamburg" with a large shipment of herring. Maybe that precious cargo is why Baruch decided that the *Prague* was right for him![16]

Whether or not Baruch and Dena initially landed in Baltimore, Baltimore is where they eventually stayed and lived their lives.

16. The Litvak fondness for herring is well known. When my father and mother married in Washington in 1950, he promised her *The New York Times* on Sundays (its only availability then outside New York, where my mom grew up), and she promised to keep herring in the refrigerator.

Image: Home bought by Baruch and Dena at 240 N. Exeter Street, Baltimore.

Source: Michael L. Millenson

242

PART TWO

Building an American Life

Baltimore Isn't New York

CHAPTER THREE

Although Baltimore, like New York, was a major port city, it was socially, culturally, and economically very different. New York even then was a large, liberal Northern metropolis. Baltimore was far smaller and more conservative, the economic center of a border state where, just 20 years earlier, Southern sympathizers had plotted to assassinate Abraham Lincoln as he traveled to his inauguration.

BEING GERMAN

Maryland ultimately did not secede from the Union. Nonetheless, its culture remained a mix of Southern (home to sprawling tobacco plantations) and Northern (a trade and manufacturing hub whose railroads served as a gateway to points west). And while there was anti-Semitism, Jews were white, a distinct benefit in the eyes of white Baltimoreans anxious about a large population of newly freed Blacks.

Baltimore's Jewish community was always much smaller than New York's. In 1900, New York had 500,000 Jews; Baltimore, around 30,000. In 1880, Baltimore had just 10,000 Jews out of a population of 382,000, or under 3 percent. By comparison, just three Lithuanian provinces contained some 400,000 Jews!

In Europe, Baruch and Dena Milenzahn were the parents of Yitzchak Leib, Yankel, and Meyer. In America, however, they could be Barnet and Annie Millenson (or sometimes Benjamin and Anna Millenson or Bernard and Deana Millenson), parents of Lou, Jack and . . . well, Meyer. (See Appendix B: The "Never-Were" Millensons, the "Almost" Millensons, and Other Genealogical Hazards.)

In Baltimore, Baruch and Dena were also part of a city where a majority of the foreign-born population spoke German, in part due to a deal between a German steamship line and the Baltimore and Ohio Railroad that spurred German immigration.[17] The German predominance in Baltimore was comfortable for the Millenson boys since they were also German—or at least often saw themselves that way.

The "German Millensons" is a concept I've struggled with. Until researching this history, I had never heard a hint of this odd self-definition. Nonetheless, Louis, Jacob, and Meyer all self-identify as German at various times, sometimes even saying that they and their parents were born there. (Other times, "Russia" remained the answer.) The boys seem to speak German, too.

Yet even if the Millenson boys spoke the language, no German Jew, much less a non-Jewish German, would ever think a Litvak was from Leipzig. So why the identification as German?

Dena's immigration record suggests that the family lived in a German-speaking area for at least five years when Louis and Jacob were young. Meyer might even have been born into that environment. Moreover, German was the language of the Enlightenment, of liberation from the strictures of the shtetl. It presented a clear contrast to speaking "Jewish" (as "Yiddish" literally means). That could be particularly attractive to a younger generation striving to carve out an identity independent of their religion.

There were other factors reinforcing an embrace of Germanness. In Baltimore, the anti-immigrant nativism of the overwhelmingly Protestant city power structure propelled the city's Jews and non-Jewish Germans into an early political alliance, note Eric L. Goldstein and Deborah R. Weiner in their book, *On Middle Ground: A History of the Jews of Baltimore.* As far back as 1843, a Lithuanian-born Jewish engraver described as "thoroughly German in cultural orientation"

17. Wikipedia. "History of the Germans in Baltimore." Accessed at: https:// en.wikipedia.org/ wiki/ History_of_the_Germans_ in_Baltimore. Also: Berman, Daphna. "A Brief History of Jewish Baltimore." *Ha'aretz*. November 13, 2012. Accessed at: https:// www.haaretz.com/ jewish/. premium-a-guide-to-jewish-baltimore-1.5197876. Also: "World Population Review: Baltimore, Maryland." Accessed at: http:// worldpopulationreview. com/us-cities/baltimore-population/

represented German Democrats at a Baltimore reception for President John Tyler.[18] We'll see later that the Millenson boys chose the same affiliation.

To be sure, the Jews didn't abandon their separate identity. What Goldstein and Weiner delicately call "acculturation" had its limits. Moreover, while the alliance between Jews and non-Jewish Germans sounds startling to us, Goldstein and Weiner point to its tangible benefits. They note that the ability of the Jewish community "to place themselves under a broader 'German' umbrella in matters of language, culture and politics, coupled with their rising economic stature, helped them gain a central role in civic life by the end of the nineteenth century."

One of the first mentions of a Millenson in America outside of a directory listing occurs in the June 4, 1886, issue of *The* (Baltimore) *Sun*, where the 21-year-old Louis is listed as the financial scribe of the new Moses Mendelson Conclave No. 29 of the Heptasophs.[19] (Jacob may have been a member, but he was not named in the article as an officer.)

The Heptasophs were a Southern fraternal organization that presented itself as a modern incarnation of the morality and virtues represented by the legends and rituals of ancient Persia and Greece. In Baltimore the group was popular among the German-speaking population. Fraternal organizations of the time served both a social and economic function, often providing financial aid to members. Crucially, the Heptasophs explicitly gave "no adherence to any religious creed . . . admitting to its mysteries both the Jew and the Christian on the common ground of mutual dependence and universal brotherhood under the Fatherhood of God," according to a contemporary account.[20]

18. Goldstein, Eric L. and Deborah R. Weiner. *On Middle Ground: A History of the Jews of Baltimore.* Baltimore: Johns Hopkins University Press, 2018

19. "Brief Locals." *The Sun*. June 4, 1886, p. 4. "Heptasophs" comes from the Greek for "Seven Wise Men." Both German and Eastern European Jews seem to have been chapter officers.

20. Stevens, Albert Clark (ed.). *The Cyclopaedia of Fraternities. A Compilation of Existing Authentic Information ....* New York: E.B. Treat and Co., 1907. p.176. Accessed at: http://bit.ly/2FIcp6R

The name chosen for the new Jewish chapter was significant. Moses Mendelssohn (the correct spelling) was a German-Jewish philosopher, an appropriate choice for the heavily German city. Perhaps more importantly, however, he was a rationalist known for urging Orthodox Jews to get "out of a ghetto lifestyle and into secular society."[21] Jews joining the Heptasophs certainly filled the bill.

In America Baruch remained deeply religious, but his sons were eager to enter the American mainstream. For Baruch's boys, that entry point was cigars.

CIGARS FOR EVERYONE

It is unclear whether Freud actually said, "Sometimes a cigar is just a cigar," although he and his circle were avid cigar smokers. However, reading Patricia Ann Cooper's 1987 book, *Once a Cigar Maker: Men, Women and Work Culture in American Cigar Factories, 1900-1919,*[22] it is clear why cigar making attracted Baruch's boys.

First, cigars were a growth industry. Cigar smoking soared in popularity in the 1870s and 1880s, supplanting snuff and other tobacco products. By 1890, the industry was turning out four billion cigars yearly, and the number of factories jumped from 4,631 in 1869 to 14,522 in 1899.

Second, barriers to entry were low. That was a major attraction for working-class young men without a lot of money or education, and neither Louis nor Jacob completed high school. As Cooper writes, "A majority of cigar manufacturers were always small shops with only a handful of workers."

Even by 1900, Cooper continues, "25 percent of U.S. production still came from shops with only one to three workers . . . [who] integrated the entire manufacturing process from preparing the raw tobacco to packing the finished cigars for shipping." These small shops were also able to sell directly to taverns and retailers; no national distribution network was needed.

21. Jewish Virtual Library. "Moses Mendelssohn, (1729-1786)." As the article notes, "Mendelssohn's own descendants, the most famous being the composer Felix Mendelssohn, left Judaism for Christianity." Accessed at: http://bit.ly/35Dp6uw

22. Cooper, Patricia Ann. *Once a Cigar Maker: Men, Women and Work Culture in American Cigar Factories, 1900-1919 (Vol. 165).* Urbana, Ill.: University of Illinois Press, 1987

A third lure for the Millenson boys may have been the expertise involved. Just as a shochet needs steady hands, dexterity, and a good eye in order to swiftly and consistently cut the carotid artery of cattle, the cigar maker must be a craftsman.

Cigar makers assembled and shaped the different components of cigars from beginning to end by themselves with the help of a few tools. A union apprenticeship could take up to three years.

"The process of making cigars involved a considerable degree of skill and experience," notes Cooper, including choosing and shaping different types of tobacco for different types of cigars whose price could sharply differ. The piecework pay depended upon the size, shape, and style of the cigars involved.

Baltimore enjoyed access both to tobacco grown in rural Maryland and to a large German population within the city. It was also home to one of the most important local chapters of the Cigar Makers International Union. That local would eventually be headed by a Jewish immigrant from England named Samuel Gompers, who would go on to found and lead the American Federation of Labor.

Unionization gave rise to a culture that likely made cigar making even more attractive to Baruch's boys. A cigar maker "was free to keep his own hours and come and go during the day," writes Cooper. The workers were engaged in skilled piecework, and "the boss did not own their time."

In sum, cigar making offered autonomy, the chance to earn good money in a growth industry, low barriers to entry, the prestige of a craftsman, and an ethnic "fit" as both Jews and Germans. We don't know when Louis and Jacob first set themselves up in the business. However, near the end of 1886, there was a fire in the oven area on the first floor of a two-story Baltimore building at 1006 Low Street rented by one "Charles Kelly" to "Lewis Millenson and Brothers" as a cigar-making facility. (Presumably, just one other brother, since Meyer was only 9 or 10 years old.) The building was located in an increasingly Jewish neighborhood that still housed Irish and Germans from previous immigration waves. Interestingly, by 1889, Baruch and family were living at 1004 Low Street, although we don't know when they moved there.[23]

23. In 1898, 12 years after the fire, Baruch buys a lot on Low Street from Charles Kelly, but we have no other information on Kelly's relationship with the Millensons.

Reports in the December 30, 1886, issues of *The Sun* and *Der Deutsche Correspondent*, a German-language Baltimore daily, disagreed about the extent of the damage and the insurance. *Der Deutsche Correspondent* said the house was insured for $1,000 and had $100 in damage but that the cigar storage area had $500 worth of damage. *The Sun* said the house was insured with Old Town Fire Insurance Company for $500, and the stock of Millenson & Co. was insured with the German-American Company for $1,000. Both articles praised the prompt response of the fire department.

Given the modest amount of equipment needed for cigar making, and that a cigar retailing for a nickel cost just a few dollars per thousand to manufacture, an insurance policy worth $500 to $1,000 appears quite substantial. In any event, the only record we have of an actual payout was $50 to L. Millenson for "fire damage" in the year ending November 30, 1899.

Although Jacob and Louis didn't succeed as cigar magnates, that wasn't unusual. In 1885, there were some 500 cigar factories in Baltimore, but just four were classified as large.[24] Writes Cooper:

> The smallest units of production were "buckeyes," which generally consisted of a lone cigar maker operating his own shop, although some included one or two journeymen. . . These rarely grew into larger enterprises and were notorious for their small financial rewards, yet their appeal lay in their clear assertion of independence. If it didn't work, you went back to the factory.

24. National Cigar History Museum. "Cigar Factories: 1885, Part II." Accessed at: http://bit.ly/2uihLUI

Image: Heineman Brothers cigar factory in 1905. Cigar makers were craftsmen who took pride in their work and dressed accordingly.

Source: Jewish Museum of Maryland

Looking for a Life Path

CHAPTER FOUR

Although all three Millenson boys started out making cigars, first Jacob, then Meyer, and at times even Louis migrated to retail. All three men would marry and have children, but Jacob would be challenged by two more store fires, while the families of Louis and Meyer would encounter unexpected tragedies whose details were definitely not something to be shared with *der kinder*.

STARTING A FAMILY

In January 1887,[25] Louis gets married in Baltimore at age 22 to Anna (Hannah) Sach, age 19, daughter of Mordecai Sach from "Russia."[26] She had come to America the previous year, possibly alone. They quickly have a son, Matthew (also known as Max), born in Baltimore on October 26, 1887.[27] A second son, Joseph, is born on April 15, 1889, also in Baltimore.[28] In 1888, Louis is listed in a Baltimore directory as a cigar maker, but in an 1890 Baltimore directory, he's a "peddler" living at 208 North Exeter Street.

By the time the couple has their third son, Samuel, on July 26, 1890, they're living in Philadelphia, a cigar-making center and Anna's home city.

Like Louis, Jacob also leaves Baltimore. He opens a clothing store in Eastville, Virginia, a tiny town perched on the far southern end of the Delmarva Peninsula. It's not long, though, before Jacob's bad luck returns. The January 11, 1889, edition of *The Sun* reports that his store "accidentally took fire tonight by the breaking of a lamp and caused a loss of about $300." Fortunately, Jacob had $1,000 worth of fire insurance. (We have no record of the actual payout.)

25. We don't have an exact date.

26. Anna's death certificate lists her mother's first name as Yente, which is also Dena Millenson's middle name, but this could be coincidence. Some family trees say her last name was Swartz, but Joseph Millenson in a bio refers to his mother's maiden name as Anna Sach.

27. Matt's World War I draft card gives his birth date as 1887; his World War II draft card says 1888. However, Baltimore Health Department records also show an October, 1887 birth.

28. As an example of varying names and spellings, Joe, born just two years later than Matt, has his parents listed on his birth certificate as Louis and Annie Millensohn, born in "Europe." Sam, born a little over a year later, is shown on a genealogy site as Samuel Milson, son of Louis and Annie Milnson.

The year 1889 was a busy one for Jacob. After the Eastville fire, he lived at least briefly in Milwaukee: "J. Millenson" is listed in the August 17, 1889, issue of the *Milwaukee Sentinel* as among those having "letters uncalled for at the Milwaukee post office." Milwaukee, of course, had a large German population, including Jews, and was a cigar-making center.

At some point Jacob must have moved to Chicago, because he was married there on February 15, 1890, at age 23, to Rebecca Rubin. This match has all the hallmarks of a "set-up."

Rebecca's father, Gerson (George), was a junk dealer born in Lithuania. Three of George's daughters married Jewish men from Baltimore, and George lived there prior to Chicago. Before Rebecca married Jacob, her younger sister Belle married Barnet (Bernard) Beneman. Beneman was a partner with and close relative of Louis Handen in a cigar-making business in Baltimore.[29] Louis Handen's wife, Anna Abramson Handen, was a niece of Baruch and was Jacob Millenson's first cousin. I'd say there's a strong probability Belle set up her sister with Anna's cousin.

29. As discussed earlier, it's unclear if this generation of Benemans and Handens were brothers or cousins.

Jacob and Rebecca are married by Rabbi Jacob Danek of Beth-El Congregation, a Conservative congregation founded by German Jews and located in a middle-class area on Chicago's North Side. In an 1890 city directory, Jacob is listed as a clerk. By the time Rebecca and Jacob's first child, George, is born on April 17, 1891, Jacob is 25 and listed on the birth certificate as being in the cigar business. Wife Rebecca, age 23, is a housewife. Both say they were born in Germany. Their address is shown only as "West Burton Place near Dearborn Parkway"—again, a middle-class area on the North Side and also an area where many German immigrants lived.

Might Jacob and Rebecca have been living in the Rubin home? Rebecca's father, Gerson, died before she gave birth to her first child; George Millenson is named after him.

Rebecca's sister, Belle Rubin Beneman, is listed on George's birth certificate as the person who delivered him. In an era without telephones, the baby may have arrived unexpectedly and forced Belle to become an emergency midwife, or it could have just been deemed a lot healthier (and less expensive) to stay far away from hospitals.

TOGETHERNESS IN CHICAGO

Chicago was experiencing an economic boom as it rebuilt from the Great Fire of 1871. By mid-1891, Louis and his family have moved to Chicago to join Jacob, according to a recently discovered timeline from their son Joe.[30] An 1892 Chicago directory lists both J. Millenson and L. Millenson as being in the cigar business and R. Millenson as a tailor. That's likely Rebecca doing sewing to earn extra money.

30. The timeline was just a few sentences of background biographical information on a job application dated 1919. That application consisted of two carbon-copy pages stapled together that were part of a sheaf of papers I inherited, since my daughter Alissa's middle name is "Joelle."

Voter rolls in 1892 show Jacob living at 34 LeMoyne Street in the less-upscale Jewish West Side, but the voter rolls don't show Louis. (The records may be incomplete.) An 1893 Chicago directory lists Romm & Millenson in the cigar business. The only Romm that I could find, Morris, was a saloon owner. It's possible his saloon was a retail outlet for their cigars.

Image: Photos of Jacob (left) and Rebecca (right) Millenson, from about 1900.

Source: Leslie Millenson Leibowitz

Separately, another directory that year reports that J. Millenson made 1,305 cigars. That modest annual total suggests someone running a cigar business rather than rolling many cigars himself.

Meanwhile, Jacob's family is growing. Rebecca gives birth to son Lester on September 7, 1894. Two years later, on September 1, 1896, son Irving is born.

The Annual Report of the Chief State Factory Inspector of Illinois for the Year Ending December 15, 1896 lists "John Millenson" (Jacob is also known as "Jack") as a cigar maker at 62 Plymouth Place. There are four employees, including one boy under age 16, one female over 16, and two males over 16.

Is Louis employed there? Perhaps. However, a report of the U.S. Industrial Commission characterizes the small cigar-making factories in Chicago as mostly "Jewish sweatshops" employing immigrants "under the most disagreeable surroundings of filth and overcrowding." That doesn't sound like an attractive workplace for a veteran craftsman, even without the additional drawback of working for his brother.

One of the few anecdotes we have about Louis also suggests he may have chosen a different workplace. At the time of the presidential election of 1896, according to a story told by my father, the foreman announced, "If McKinley doesn't win, don't bother coming into work." (William McKinley was the Republican candidate.) Louis promptly went out and voted for William Jennings Bryan, the Democrat. Luckily for Louis's continued employment, McKinley triumphed anyway.

Apprentices in cigar manufacturing, writes Cooper, began working between the ages of 14 and 16. She adds, "In Chicago the apprentices usually made the cheapest five-cent cigars while they were learning, and they were often expected to smoke their own cigars to test how good a product they were making." This is pretty much what's happening to Meyer, except in Baltimore.

An 1893 Baltimore directory lists "Meyer Milenson," then 15 or 16, as a cigar maker at 914 East Baltimore Street. That year Meyer's cousin Charles, son of Tsvi Hirsch and Rachael Abramson, also works in the cigar business. (See Appendix C: The Abramson Connection.)

Image: George, Irving, and Lester Millenson, c. 1900

Source: John Lowenberg

Meyer appears in an 1895 Baltimore directory and is an usher at a friend's wedding in Baltimore in February 1896. However, two of Meyer's daughters later recalled that he moved to Chicago around 1894 or 1895 to join his two brothers and to enroll in college.[31]

Louis, Jacob, and Meyer are all short (5'3" or so), solidly built, and sport moustaches. The older two likely had a distinct Yiddish accent to their speech in a way that distinguished them from their youngest sibling. But the brothers' togetherness in Chicago doesn't last. After one semester Meyer drops out of school because of respiratory issues and decides to move to Denver for its clean mountain air. Family stories say Meyer contracted tuberculosis (TB) and took many months to recover.

In any event, the three brothers would never again live in the same place.

31. One daughter recalled "college," another "Northwestern Law School." Northwestern could not confirm Meyer's attendance at any part of the school.

Image: Map of Jewish East Baltimore

Source: Jewish Museum of Maryland

Baruch & Dena

CHAPTER FIVE

We know very little about the daily lives of Baruch and Dena Millenson. But we can perhaps get a few glimpses into who they were based on snippets of information and some digging into historical context.

BUTCHER, PEDDLER, AND RABBI

It is the early 1880s in Harrisburg, a river-and-railroad hub chosen as Pennsylvania's state capital more than 70 years before, yet still lacking even one paved street. The police have been called in to break up a fight with familiar antagonists: the town's tiny Orthodox Jewish community, which has become infamous for periodic brawls.One of the men the police find on the scene (bystander? participant? instigator? peacemaker?) is also familiar, a 40-something local who non-Jews know by various names but the other Jews know as "Baruch."

While this scenario is admittedly not based on an actual incident, it's also not just pure speculation. The Jewish community of Harrisburg is, to say the least, interesting, even though there are just a few hundred Jewish residents.[32] For instance, some reportedly found their way there unintentionally when, riding the Pennsylvania Railroad and speaking only Yiddish, they were advised by a Jewish interpreter that the Harrisburg stop was where they should get off.

32. Benson, Arlene. "The Jewish Residents of Harrisburg's Old Eighth Ward and Adjacent Neighborhoods: 1860-1924." The Pennsylvania State University at Harrisburg. May 2008. Accessed at: http://bit.ly/3at1ziA. Other information from Ancestry.com.

The initial Jewish immigrants are less-observant German Jews, but the number of Eastern European Jews from a more-traditional background is growing by the time Baruch arrives. Although the community is small, it has still managed to split into a Reform faction, meeting at its own building with its own rabbi, and a less-numerous Orthodox group clustered for prayer services at the home of Hyman Klaster, a Lithuanian-born merchant.

The first inkling we have of where Baruch Millenson is living in America and what he's doing comes from the *1883 Boyd's Harrisburg and Steelton Directories.* It mentions a "Bernard Mellinson" living at 430 South Avenue in Harrisburg and working as a butcher. That same year the Orthodox group in Harrisburg decides to start their own synagogue, and they appoint a six-person committee to draw up a congregational constitution. The committee is chaired by a man who formerly smuggled goods between Lithuania and the German towns just over the border.[33]

Even among this small group of Orthodox Jews, there's still room enough for serious disagreements. Four committee members, including the chair, are among the 13 men who sign the founding document of Congregation Chisuk Emunah (Strength of Faith). However, two committee members, Louis Potts and "Benjamin Millinson," do not.

The strength of the faith that the men of Chisuk Emunah place in their own opinions often seems to rival the strength of their religious faith, and not all disagreements are peaceful. As a history of the congregation phrased it, "The Orthodox in Harrisburg had a reputation for brawling. By universal repute, the police had to be called in to break up fracases on crucial occasions."

We don't know the extent to which Baruch was battler or bystander. We do know, though, that hard feelings from the constitutional conclave didn't linger between Baruch and a young shul founder who did sign the document. When Isaac Klaster, Hyman's 23-year-old son, marries his cousin Esther Klaster, Baruch plays a prominent role. The December 12, 1884, ceremony is the first Jewish wedding in Harrisburg—or "Russian-Hebrew wedding," as local newspapers put it. *The Telegraph* describes an elegant ceremony at the home of the bridegroom's parents, where "the parlors were elaborately decorated in silk," and prominent local Gentile citizens joined the assembled Hebrews.[34]

33. The information on Harrisburg's Orthodox community comes from scholar Bruce Bazelon.

34 "A Novel Wedding: A Russian-Hebrew Marriage Takes Place in this City." *The* (Harrisburg) *Patriot*, December 13, 1834, p. 1. While the reporter was vague about the groom's age and appearance, he was a keener observer of one of the bridesmaids, whom he characterized as "a beautiful brunette of petite figure, large lustrious [cq] eyes and fine dark hair falling gracefully over her shoulders."

A page-one story in *The Patriot* delved into even greater detail about the rites "solemnized by Rabbi Millenson, of this city, assisted by Rabbi Trone, recently arrived here from Russia." Guests were treated to wine, Russian cakes, and sweetmeats. The bride entered with her bridesmaids and friends carrying lighted candles. A "beautiful glass chalice was filled with wine," and one of the rabbis chanted "a portion of the Hebrew marriage ritual." Wine was offered to the couple, the groom slipped the wedding ring onto the bride's finger, and Rabbi Millenson then "produced a few pages of foolscap written in Hebrew and read their marriage contract." (Presumably, the contract was actually written in the traditional Aramaic.) The groom and bride then drank the wine, after which Rabbi Millenson "threw the vessel upon the floor, stamping upon it with his feet and crushing it to atoms. This ended the ceremony."

While shochets were often rabbis and cantors, and one of Baruch's grandchildren heard him described as "a teacher of rabbis," this account confirms that Baruch was, indeed, not only a rabbi but likely the only Orthodox rabbi in Harrisburg for several years.

An 1885 directory shows a B. Millenson still living in Harrisburg and selling notions. There's also an unclaimed letter for him in December of that year at the Baltimore post office, the city to which Baruch and Dena return by 1886. They may have been unhappy with their economic prospects in Harrisburg, uneasy about the chances of living an observant Jewish family life there, or had other reasons we'll never know. Although Baruch's name subsequently begins to show up in Baltimore directories as a butcher, another decade passes before he's once more in the news. This time, though, it's not as clergy but in a courtroom.

A SOLDIER IN THE "KOSHER MEAT WAR"

As the 20th century neared, difficult conditions in the Pale sparked an outpouring of emigrants. As the demand for kosher meat increased, so did prices, to such an extent that they set the stage for an intense and years-long communal conflict among immigrants in multiple cities. In Baltimore an early clash centered on who was qualified to ritually slaughter cattle.

What would come to be called the "kosher meat war" provides an unexpected glimpse into Baruch's work as a shochet.

The Jewish Museum of Maryland described the background: In 1896, one Herman Schwartzberg drew up a contract between a kosher butcher in Baltimore, Levy Edlavitch, and a shochet, Isaac Salowitschick, for the latter to slaughter cattle for the former at a fixed price per animal. Edlavitch ended his agreement with Salowitschick after two local Orthodox rabbis claimed that the shochet was not competent to carry out his duties. Only if the shochet brought a certificate from the [correct] rabbis would the butcher retain the shochet.

> The dismissed shochet promptly sued the butcher in local court for breach of contract, asserting that he was both competent and certified by a recognized rabbinic authority . . . . Three expert shochets testified in court on the rules of *schechita* (ritual slaughter) and on the matter of rabbinic authority.[35]

One of the rabbis testifying against Salowitschick revealed that local rabbis had published a list of "recognized" shochets in order to restrict entry into the field, "as there was not enough work to support all who might wish to engage in it." This led Salowitschick's lawyer to charge that a "combine" was trying to control all kosher slaughtering.

35. Decter, Avi Y. "Processions, Debates and Curbstone Encounters: The Struggle over Kosher Meat in Baltimore, 1897-1918, Pt. 2." Jewish Museum of Maryland. 2017. Accessed at: http://bit.ly/ 31qfOkT

The evidence suggests he had a point. As the Jewish Museum history points out, the shochets were employed by the wholesale butchers. Those butchers, in turn, depended upon the *kashrut* approval of certain powerful rabbis. So it's perhaps unsurprising that the three "expert shochets" all testified that Edlavitch, presumably their employer, was justified in breaking his contract with Salowitschick.

One of those experts was Baruch.

The trial, wrote *The Sun*, drew "a large audience of orthodox and liberal Jews." The newspaper did its part to maintain public interest among gentiles, headlining its April 6, 1897, story: "Mosaic Butchering. Ancient Levitical Laws Regarding Cattle-Killing Aired in Court. Schochets' Cholofs Flash. The Sharp Knives Figure in Realistic Testimony." (A *cholof* was the knife used for ritual slaughter.)

The Sun translation of schochet (their spelling) was not "ritual slaughterer" but "killer," as in, "One of the exhibits in the case is the knife used by the killer."

Baruch was not named by *The Sun*, but his testimony about Salowitschick's fitness for the job was cited in *Der Deutsche Correspondent*—which was how, early in my research, Baruch's occupation was discovered for the first time. A German-born member of my synagogue translated the passage this way:

> Baruch Millenson, an expert shochet, declared on the witness stand that he did not see how the accuser killed cattle. He submitted that the knife was not long enough, in this land in which cattle were bigger than in Europe, to use it for the Israelite custom.

The court eventually ruled in favor of Salowitschick. As to whether the knife was really too short, note that Baruch opined that the knife's size was inadequate, but he did not testify under oath that he'd actually seen Salowitschick having any difficulty slaughtering cattle.

Controversy over the power of the rabbinate and the high price of kosher meat continued in Baltimore, New York, and elsewhere, at times prompting strikes, boycotts, and even riots by angry Jewish housewives. ("Butcher Shops in Philadelphia Were Sacked By Yiddish Mobs" read one 1907 headline.) To what extent Baruch was affected is unclear, but he was listed in Baltimore directories as a butcher as late as 1908, the year of his death.

Image: The Yiddish sign, "shochet" (kosher butcher) is transliterated here into "Schechter" someone who "schechts" (koshers) meat.

Source: Jewish Museum of Maryland, Jacques Kelly Collection

A BRUTAL ATTACK ON BARUCH

What caused Morris (Max) Shapiro to brutally beat Baruch Millenson, a man more than 30 years his senior, in 1903? Shapiro was a tailor. Baruch owned property. Was this a tenant/landlord dispute? Was some other grudge involved? Whatever the cause, this was no casual outburst.

In a lawsuit filed on May 27, 1903, Baruch sought $10,000 in damages, or nearly $300,000 in today's dollars. The complaint charges that "Shapero" (as the name is misspelled) "beat [Baruch] and with great force and violence struck . . . numerous portions of his . . . face and head." The beating left Baruch "sick, sore, lame and disordered and so continued for a great length of time."

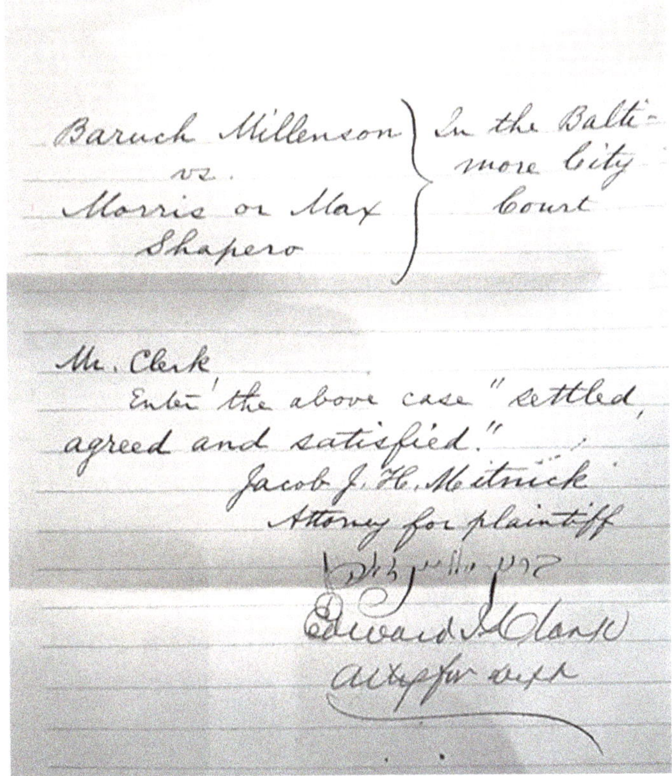

Baruch Millenson vs. Morris or Max Shapero } In the Baltimore City Court

Mr. Clerk
Enter the above case "settled, agreed and satisfied."
Jacob J. H. Mitnick
Attorney for plaintiff

Edward J. Clark
atty for deft

Image: Baruch's signature in Yiddish on a personal injury lawsuit he filed in 1904.

Source: Maryland State Archives

Baruch, the complaint continued, "suffered great pain," could not attend to his work or other affairs of life and was forced to "expend a large sum of money" on medical care. Even so, he remained "permanently injured in his health and his capacity for earning a livelihood has thereby been permanently impaired." Baruch's lawsuit lists eight witnesses, including his brother, to back up his case.

Why didn't Baruch call the police? Several possible reasons come to mind. Not only was Baruch a badly injured man in his mid-60s, dazed and worried, but it is unclear how quickly one could find a police call box in that era and how quickly help would arrive. It's also unclear how well Baruch spoke English: in the legal complaint, he signs his name in Yiddish. Moreover, a Jewish immigrant from czarist Russia might well have hesitated about turning a fellow Jew over to uniformed, non-Jewish police.

Finally, given Baruch's exposure to routine physical violence in Europe, Harrisburg, and possibly in Baltimore's immigrant community, he may not have been totally blameless in whatever caused the dispute to escalate.

Did Shapiro even have $10,000? It's doubtful, but in any event, the economy of Baltimore was staggered less than a year after the lawsuit was filed by the Great Fire of February 7–8, 1904. The fire destroyed much of central Baltimore and more than 1,000 buildings overall in a burned-out area stretching for 140 acres. On February 2, 1905, *The Sun* reported that Baruch's lawsuit had been settled but gave no details.[36]

Baruch undoubtedly suffered lingering physical, economic, and psychological effects from this assault, but they remain unknown.

36. The one-line item in the February 2, 1905, edition of *The Sun* is part of a list of judicial actions. It not only erroneously characterizes Baruch as the defendant, but it botches both his first and last names. The case is presented as "Max Shapero vs. Baroux Millinson."

THE LAST YEARS

In the crowded Jewish neighborhood where Baruch and Dena lived, there was a wide variety of nearby synagogues to choose from. The couple may have *davened* (prayed) at a number of different shuls, but what's particularly interesting is where they went toward the end of Baruch's life.

The cemetery where Baruch is buried was owned by a synagogue founded in 1890 by Jews with both German and Eastern European names and with working-class jobs like tailor, peddler, and grocer. German and Eastern European Jews had very different customs, so this commonality was unusual. But even more eyebrow-raising was that the synagogue was the first Lubavitcher Hasid shul in Baltimore.

Baruch, an Orthodox rabbi from the heartland of Lithuanian rationalism, a tradition whose deep antipathy to Hasidism led to Litvaks being called "*misnagdim*" (opponents), belonged to Anshe Niezen Nusach Ari. This was a shul named in honor of both a Hasidic rabbi and a 16th century Jewish mystic.[37]

Anshe Niezen (sometimes spelled "Niesen" or "Neisen") was initially located in the Carroll Mansion, a dwelling of the old Maryland elite that, according to an 1895 visitor, was now part of a Jewish "slum." An article in *The Sun* told of a junk shop on the ground floor, while the Hasidic congregation worshipped in the "faded parlor." Most congregants had fled pogroms in the Ukrainian town of Nizhyn, home of an early Lubavitcher rabbi. "Russian" families "with their broods" filled the building, and "Yiddish was a dominant tongue."[38]

37. Anshe Niezen Nusach Ari translates as "The Men of Niezen Who Follow the Customs of the 'Ari,'" a 16th-century Jewish mystic and rabbi in Safed.

38. The mansion, at 800 E. Lombard Street, was named for Charles Carroll of Carrollton, a signer of the Declaration of Independence. The renovated mansion is now promoted as an "urban oasis." Accessed at: https://www.carrollmuseums.org/explore/carroll-mansion/

A clue as to how Baruch could have found it acceptable to belong to this shul comes from Katz's book on Lithuanian Jewry. In Lithuania, years of conflict pitted followers of the Gaon of Vilna against Hasidim who proclaimed that their rabbis were "miracle workers." But then the Lubavitcher rabbi Schneur-Zalman began to create a different kind of Hasidism. It was "a new branch of Lithuanian Jewish culture that fused the Lithuanian passion for learning with a moderated form of Hasidic life and lore."

The name that Schneur-Zalman chose for his movement, Chabad, represented an acronym taken from three of the ten *sfirot* (spheres) that mystics say represent the "emanations" of God. This, concludes Katz, was a statement at the popular level that the Chabad branch of Hasidism stood for wisdom,understanding, and knowledge. It was "an assurance to scholars of the Gaon's ilk that there is frankly nothing to worry about."[39]

This calming approach was sufficiently effective that there were shtetls populated mostly by Hasidim that had non-Hasidic rabbis and vice versa. Perhaps that was even the case in Grinkishok or some of the nearby villages.

Baruch died from "paralysis" on the morning of October 14, 1908, at the Bay View Hospital and Asylum. (Bay View served the poor; the word "asylum" meant "refuge.") He was buried in the Anshe Niezen cemetery. His death certificate shows that his tombstone bears the correct Hebrew date but an incorrect English date of September 14. The English spells his first name as "Burech," likely based on the Yiddish pronunciation.[40]

39. Pietella, Antero. *The Ghosts of Johns Hopkins: The Life and Legacy that Shaped an American City.* Baltimore: Rowland & Whittlefield, 2018. p. 120. Accessed at: http://bit.ly/37qZiD7. My thanks to Chabad of Baltimore for providing historical background.

40. The executor for the estate of Baruch, a kosher slaughterer, was Louis Hollander, who was a cattle-feed salesman.

"Millenson" is spelled out in one of its Yiddish versions. (They varied.) The two large Hebrew letters at the top are an abbreviation for "Here is Buried." The inscription in Hebrew reads, "Here lies a modest and honest man, our teacher the Rav Baruch, son of Reb Nachum Millenson, who died on 18 Tishrei 5668." The Hebrew letters at the bottom are an abbreviation for "May his soul be bound up in eternal life." ("Reb" is an honorific, not an indication that someone was a rabbi, but the Hebrew abbreviation for the phrase translated as "our teacher the rav" typically is.)

Whatever Baruch's rough edges, this respectful description of him seems to have been wholly appropriate.

Dena lived almost a dozen years more than her husband, dying on the evening of July 13, 1920, according to her death certificate. (It was after sunset, so the Hebrew date corresponds to July 14). Her will was handwritten by someone else and signed by her with an "X" as "her mark." It also calls her "Annie Millison."[41]

Dena divided up her property among her sons and grandchildren and also gave them most of the cash that would remain after funeral expenses. However, she also left money to a Jewish home for the aged as well as to two Orthodox yeshivas.

That last gift may provide another indication of how Baruch and Dena transcended typical community divisions. A few years earlier, one of the yeshivas had introduced English as a language of instruction. A break-off group promptly founded a rival yeshiva dedicated to teaching "the principles of Orthodox Judaism in Yiddish."[42] Dena donated to both.

41. Making this even more confusing is another Baltimore Jewish family named "Millison."

42. op. cit., Goldstein and Weiner

Dena's death certificate says she died of chronic nephritis, an infection that can cause kidney failure, at Springfield State Hospital. The hospital was located on a former private estate in Sykesville that had been turned into a state-run psychiatric facility. She was there for three and a half months, suggesting she suffered from what we'd call dementia and what was then called "senile debility."

Dena's tombstone, a more-polished "upgrade" over Baruch's stone a dozen years before, says in English, "D. Millenson." Inside a Jewish star at the top is once again the Hebrew abbreviation for "Here is Buried." The brief inscription in Hebrew reads, "Our dear mother, Marat (an honorific for a married woman) Dena Yenta, Crown of Tsvi (a reference to her piety), 28 Tammuz 5679." This is followed by the Hebrew abbreviation for "May her soul be bound up in eternal life."

As dedicated as Dena was to *Yiddishkeit*, by the time she dies, her sons are living very American lives.

Image: Tombstones of Baruch Millenson (left) from 1908, with an incorrect English month of death, and Dena Millenson (right), from 1920, with no English dates at all.

Source: FindAGrave.com

On the Move

CHAPTER SIX

The Panic of 1893, which led to the Depression of 1893 to 1897, hit industrial cities particularly hard. By 1898, the Millensons have left Chicago, and each brother has started to define his own life path. Louis initially moves back to Philadelphia, Jacob heads back to the Delmarva Peninsula, and Meyer sets his sights on Denver.

LOUIS'S PAINFULLY PUBLIC MARITAL PROBLEMS

Louis's family moves back to Philadelphia in April 1898, according to Joe's timeline. Did Annie want to return to her roots for economic and emotional support? In the 1900 Census, Louis and Annie report having had five children, but they say that only three survived.[44]

44. We have a birth certificate for one of the children who did not survive, Nathan.

Although Louis is shown as living in Philadelphia in the 1900 Census and in a 1901 directory, it's unclear how much time he spent there. Modern DNA analysis reveals that in early 1899 he and the equally married (and Catholic) Mary Catherine Porter Eisenhauer conceived a child in Baltimore. Separately, long-forgotten letters to a Yiddish newspaper, discovered during this research, shine a harsh light on the deep troubles in Louis Millenson's marriage.

Louis Paul Eisenhauer was born to Mary Catherine and Stephen Eisenhauer on December 1, 1899. Like the Millensons, the Eisenhauers already had three children. Despite some family suspicions, proof of Louis Eisenhauer's out-of-wedlock status, or "misattributed parentage," was only discovered in 2019 by his granddaughter Rachel Eisenhauer via genetic testing. The Ashkenazi Jewish genes in Rachel's DNA matched most closely with DNA from Millenson descendants.

How did Mary Catherine and Louis meet? Although an 1897 Denver directory lists Meyer working there as a clerk, giving credence to the story that he went west due to respiratory problems, an 1899 Baltimore directory lists "Myer Millenson" as a grocer at 2201 East Fayette Street. That address is not far from the Eisenhauer home. A family story says Meyer returned to Baltimore after recuperating from TB because of a girl to whom he was engaged, only to find that during his absence she had become engaged to someone else. Perhaps during Meyer's sojourn back in Baltimore he worked as a grocer (certainly not in cigars!), and Louis sometimes joined him at the store.

Or perhaps Louis and Mary Catherine's husband met through the Heptasophs. Or perhaps Louis was the mysterious "Egyptian tobacconist" boarder that Eisenhauer family lore says lived in their home. Just for the heck of it, I'd like to say Louis and Mary Catherine's bond began over a shared enthusiasm for high-quality household supplies.

While we don't know how the two met or what attracted each to the other, we do know that Mary Catherine had lost a five-year old daughter in August 1898 and that Louis also had the experience of losing a child. It's likely each was unhappy in their marriages.

In any event, by the summer of 1901, Louis was not living at home. We know this from the Personal Column of the newspaper *Yiddishes Tageblatt* (*The Jewish Daily News*). The painful correspondence between Louis and his children was mentioned in a footnote by Caroline Light in a book chapter examining the abandonment of wives in the Jewish community during this time period. Although the wives saw their absent husbands as irresponsible, the men (and some women) blamed the wives for making home life unbearable.[45] Light's footnote led to me tracking down the July 12, 1901, issue of the *Tageblatt*.

45. Personal correspondence with Caroline E. Light, February 1, 2020, and Chapter 4 of her book *The Pride of Race and Character: The Rootsof Jewish Benevolence in the Jim Crow South*. New York: NYU Press, 2014

A "personal ad" from "Louie's" three children on that date, and his response on July 14, with the children's original plea re-published above it, are emotionally difficult to read even now. After locating microfilm of the newspaper with Caroline's help, I had the letters translated by a professional.[46] The awkward language reflects the Yiddish original.

46. Translation by J. Felendler, March 18, 2020

Here's the letter from the children:

> Philadelphia. We are looking for our father Louie Millenson, a cigar maker, 37 years old, he left us along with our sick mother on the 17th of May without [even] a cent of money. He promised us that he'd write to us immediately and he had said that he's leaving to peddle. However, we found out that he had gathered money by his cousin in order to be able to leave us. His father, Boruch Millenson, a shochet in Baltimore, had talked him into it that he is too weak to support us in order that he should leave us. It's said that he had sent him for pleasure and we're dying here of hunger. We're begging our father he should have mercy on us and our sick mother with whom he's married already for 15 years, he should send us at least something with which to live, because we are in great need. We are living on the 3rd floor in one room, hungry and miserable. Your children, Max, Joe and Sam. 404 South 6th St., Philadelphia, Pa.

Image: Mary Catherine Porter Eisenhauer in 1950 at age 79.

Source: Rachel Eisenhauer

And here's the response:

> My dear children! You don't need to look for me. I didn't run away neither from you or your mother. Had your mother not made me leave home I wouldn't have done it myself for luxury. I didn't leave to search for pleasures but rather work. I am in Chicago and I'm working at all times. If your mother will be pleased with how much I earn, and not hidden away in separate knots [an idiomatic Yiddish expression for hidden money, practically done by knotting it away as a means of hiding], yet rather to be devoted as a wife [should be] to a husband, she could come along with all of you and you all won't be lacking anything. Don't let her throw the blame at my family. Your devoted father, Louie Millenson.

Are the kids accusing Baruch of telling Louis to leave and have a good time? Or did Baruch tell his son he needed to either find a way to support his family in Philadelphia or go elsewhere and figure it out? Since, as we'll see in a moment, Louis waited to divorce Anna until Baruch died, I think the latter is more likely. The phrase "It's said" apparently refers to rumors about why Louis left. It's certainly possible that his dalliance with Mary Catherine, and perhaps others, was a poorly kept secret.

Louis responds that he's working hard in Chicago, and if Mom will stop hiding money (because she doesn't trust him?) and be a devoted wife (a phrase that is sometimes a coded reference to marital relations), everything will be fine. There is no identification of which Abramson cousin gave Louis money, nor any explanation as to why Louis is not sending money home to support his family if he's doing so well in Chicago.

Image: From left, Joseph, Samuel, and Max (Matt) Millenson in an undated photo from about 1893.

Source: Michael M. Millenson

In that era before telephones or reliable postal service, the Yiddish press played a central role in the American Jewish community. *Yiddishes Tageblatt* was the first daily Yiddish paper in the world and stridently Orthodox. What did it mean to have one's family troubles prominently displayed in its pages?

PERSONAL COLUMN.

פערזענליכעס — פערזענליכעס.

Image: Ad in the July 12, 1901, *Yiddishes Tageblatt* by "Louie" Millenson's three sons, asking for help finding him and pleading for him to return.

Source: Hebrew Union College—Jewish Institute of Religion

In July of 1901 my grandfather Joe was just 12 years old, his younger brother, Sam, was 11, and his older brother, Max (Matt), was turning 14. Years later, without mentioning his father's abandonment, Joe would talk about dropping out of school and selling newspapers on the street and working odd jobs to help support his family.

In 1988, Matt's widow, Rose Greinitz Millenson, remembered how her late husband described the relationship between Anna, the only child of an Orthodox rabbi, and Louis. "Matt always said that his mother was crazy clean and Orthodox crazy, and Lou didn't want that. She was too religious."

Whatever the specifics regarding Louis, many cigar makers were wanderers. "In any given year in the early 20th century, one third or more of union members left home to travel and work elsewhere," writes Cooper. "Travel was so much a part of the work lives of members that they sometimes referred to their union as the 'traveling fraternity.'" Issues of their journal would include names of those who owed money or whose wives were trying to find out where they were.

And they weren't the only ones. Desertion was nicknamed "the poor man's divorce," and Jews were not immune to its lure. In 1902, the National Council of Jewish Charities created a Department of Desertion that grew in a little over a decade into a National Desertion Bureau and then into an independent organization. By the mid-1920s, the Yiddish newspaper *Forvert* was regularly publishing photos of "a gallery of missing husbands."[47]

47. "Jewish Genealogy: What Are They Hoping to Find?" *Tablet*, November 12, 2020

In the June 1903 *Cigar Makers Official Journal*, Louis is listed as a new union member in Chicago. (New? And in Chicago? One more mystery.) Finally, in 1905, he's listed as a cigar maker at Winter Cigar Manufacturing Co. in Denver. By that year Meyer is back in Denver and is married. Jacob, meanwhile, is firmly anchored as a prototypical Jewish mer chant in small-town America.

JACOB AND THE "JEW STORE"

Unlike Louis, when Jacob left Chicago he also left cigars firmly behind. By the 1890s, he's back on the Delmarva Peninsula, this time farther north in the tiny town of East New Market, Maryland.

Jacob's in-laws, Barnet and Belle Beneman, owned a store in St. Michael's. Other Jewish immigrants were starting to follow a similar path to the peninsula. It was a time when "almost every town of any size in Maryland and Virginia contains one or more Russian [Jewish] store-keepers," according to a contemporary report cited by Goldstein and Weiner.

A 1902 description of East New Market by a longtime resident depicted a "thriving village" of about 600 inhabitants, surrounded by "some of the best farmland in the county" for fruits and vegetables. Two railroad lines served the area, and daily steamship service to Baltimore was available on a Choptank River tributary nearby. The Benemans no doubt recommended the town to Jacob and Rebecca, perhaps adding a few words about weather and lifestyle advantages compared to Chicago.

In her book, *The Jew Store: A Family Memoir*, Stella Stuberman tells how her father ended up as a merchant in a small Southern town. Although the town was very small, "it was actually larger than the town in which he grew up," a shtetl in Russia. They were the only Jewish family, but Stuberman notes that her father "really didn't take religion seriously." He had no problem working Saturdays and closing on Sundays.[48]

This description seems a perfect fit for Jacob.

An article in the *American Jewish Year Book* calculated the Maryland Jewish population in 1902 based on a mailed survey to officials outside Baltimore asking, "How many Jews live in your village or county?" (!) The author found a total of 1,500 non-Baltimore Jews, with the largest group being 165 Jews living in Cumberland. There were five in East New Market.[49] Those were the Millensons.

In the 1900 Census, the Millenson household consisted of Jacob, Rebecca, and their three sons (ages nine, six and four) and two others. One was Nancy Mathews, age 21, a Black "servant"—presumably live-in childcare. There was also Michael Fox, age 14, listed as a stock clerk.[50] "Fox" was Rebecca's mother's maiden name (Ida Fox Rubin), and Michael was a cousin. (Perhaps because he was not a permanent resident, Michael was not included in the Jewish resident head count.)

Still, if Baltimore wasn't New York, East New Market could not have presented a starker contrast to Chicago. Less than 40 years earlier, traders from Delaware and New Jersey met in the town "to sell negroes or exchange horses," the 1902 account noted. It added: "Iron staples are still shown here in one building to which slave negroes were chained for safe keeping" until sold or conveyed farther south.[51]

48. Stuberman, Stella. *The Jew Store*. Chapel Hill, NC: Algonquin Books, 2001

49. Barnett, George E. "The Jewish Population of Maryland." In *American Jewish Year Book, 1899-2008*. Springer: American Jewish Committee. Accessed at: http://bit.ly/2sGD9lE

50. The census lists them as Willinson or Millinson. Michael Fox is "Michel" Fox.

51. Jacobs, Pink. "East NewMarket." In *A History of Dorchester County. Baltimore*, by Elias Jones. Williams& Wilkins Company Press, 1902

Image: Postcard of Millenson Department Store in East New Market, Maryland, in 1916.

Source: East New Market Fire Company Archives

The town and the Millenson Department Store (also known as J. Millenson and Son) prospered, and Jacob soon became part of the community's social fabric. Newspaper articles tell of his participation in the Woodrow Wilson Progressive League, local parades, and the Pomona Grange Exhibition. In that last event, held in October 1913, the "large number of handsome prizes" included $2.50 in gold to the exhibitor of the best white sweet potatoes, courtesy of the East New Market Bank, while the runner-up received a "large velvet rug" donated by J. Millenson. And when, in 1915, East New Market forms a Chamber of Commerce (then called a "board of trade") with some 100 members, Jacob is part of the executive committee.

Jacob also owned or had an interest in a tomato cannery, according to one family story, at a time when the Delmarva Peninsula boasted of being "The Tomato Canning Capital of the World." Meanwhile, Jacob's younger brother, Meyer, was having a much tougher time in retail in Denver.

MEYER'S DRAMA IN DENVER

The Jewish population of Denver had begun to grow in the mid-1800s as mining for gold and other minerals attracted fortune seekers. Still, before 1900, Colorado had just 1,500 Jews out of a total state population of about 540,000. By 1907, however, the Jewish population had soared to about 7,000, with some 5,000 of that number living in Denver.[52]

It wasn't just economic opportunity that attracted new residents. By the late 1890s, refugees from America's polluted industrial cities were flocking to Denver to escape allergies and "the white plague," as TB (tuberculosis) or "consumption" was called. The National Jewish Hospital for Consumptives opened in 1899, and the Jewish Consumptives Relief Society was formed in 1904. At the time, TB was the third most common cause of death in America after cardiovascular diseases and influenza/pneumonia.[53]

Just as the Baltimore of 1880 had not yet shed the influence of the Civil War, the Denver where Meyer settled was replete with reminders of the Wild West. Although Denver offered clear mountain air, an article in *The Denver Post* on October 31, 1901, relates a different health hazard that Meyer faced as a driver for a meat and grocery store. [54] The newspaper paints a scene straight out of a dime-store novel:

> Out near the Jewish hospital, where Colfax Avenue becomes an almost deserted lane, two highwaymen with drawn revolvers robbed Meyer Millenson of $100 Tuesday evening.

52. Abrams, Jeanne. "Jewish Denver: 1859-1940." Cited in Denverite.com, October 5,2017. Accessed at: http://bit.ly/2sWQeHz

53. Murray, John F. "A Century of Tuberculosis," *American Journal of Respiratory and Critical CareMedicine*. 2004. 169(11):1181-1186. Accessed at: http://bit.ly/2FrIFdW

54. Blakemore, Erin. "The Disease That Helped Put Colorado on the Map." History (Channel). Accessed at: http://bit.ly/2t2QMM8

> The day had turned to dusk and Millenson, who is a collector and driver for the Otto Shatz Grocery company, was returning to the city after a fairly successful day's work . . . . Just beyond the hospital two men sprung into the road suddenly, and one seized the bridle of the nearest horse. The barrels of two pistols glistened as both men drew.
>
> "Shell out yer dough, young feller. Every cent of it," said one, sharply. "And be – – – – quick about it, too," exclaimed the other, roughly.
>
> They thrust their leveled guns toward Millenson's head. There was but one thing to do, and he did it.

After Meyer forked over the cash, the robbers held him at gunpoint while they started his team of horses down the road. Once the horses had disappeared, the men let him go alone into the night. After catching up with the"faithful, puzzled animals," Millenson drove back into town.[55]

55. "Poke Guns in His Face. Bold Robbers Hold Up Grocer's Driver." *The Denver Post* October 31, 1901, p. 8. Later articles will use this robbery and others as evidence of a crime spree enabled by a weak police force whose ranks were filled with political appointees rather than professionals.

In the 1902 Denver directory, Meyer has given up driving for Shatz and is listed as a "clerk."

On March 27, 1904, a few weeks before Meyer turns 27, he marries Theresa Prussick, 28, in Denver. (She's also known as Pruscik/Prusick/Prusic.) Meyer had been a boarder in the home of Theresa's mother, according to Rose Millenson, a native Denverite whose family knew both Meyer and Theresa. Meanwhile, Louis, his marriage on the rocks, was also interested in Theresa, both Rose and one of Meyer's daughters later recalled.

Meyer and Theresa's marriage certificate, signed by Rabbi H. Ovsovitz, a Russian-born Orthodox rabbi, shows this was a second marriage for Prussick, but that's only a hint of Theresa's colorful past. This was no cousin from the shtetl.

Theresa was born in Liverpool, England, to a Russian-Jewish family who immigrated to America in 1878. Theresa, two sisters, her mother, and a brother traveled by oxcart to the Colorado Territory around 1891, and the children were educated at a convent school. On January 1, 1900, when Theresa was only 22, she married a Jewish man six years older, Ellis Gerson. Together, according to family stories, they ran away to a circus in Tarrytown, New York.

On Theresa and Meyer's marriage certificate, she lists herself as having been divorced in 1902. In response to the question, "On what grounds?" she answers, "Do not know." Meanwhile, the name "Theresa Prusick" with the occupation of "seamstress," appears periodically in Denver directories from1895 through 1905.

Meyer and Theresa had twin baby girls, born prematurely, who died on October 19, 1904. A year later, on October 10, 1905, the couple has their first child who survived, Nathan David Millenson, likely named in honor of Meyer's grandfather Nahum.

Baruch, as noted above, died in Baltimore on October 14, 1908. After his death, everything changed.

Life Paths Diverge

CHAPTER SEVEN

On October 27, 1908, just two weeks after Baruch's death, Louis files for divorce from Hannah/Anna/Edna in a Denver court. She's still living in Philadelphia. At the time, she's supporting herself, according to a directory, by doing "trimmings," or sewing finishing details on clothing.

On October 30 in Denver, Meyer and Theresa have a daughter they name Libby Leah after Theresa's mother and Meyer's grandmother.

EXPANSION

At the time Meyer starts his family, he is working as a driver for the Colorado Hand Laundry, a job that involves being paid pennies per pound on commission for heavy loads of wash collected in horse-drawn carts. Meanwhile, his brother Louis suddenly acquires an entire second family.

On June 15, 1909, Louis marries another Anna, the widow Anna Bennett, also known as Annie, just as his first wife was. They are wed in a civil ceremony in the town of Goodland, Kansas, just east of the Colorado border, for reasons that are unclear.[56] Perhaps Louis did not yet have a religious divorce from his first wife, or perhaps Louis and/or Anna Bennett didn't care much about religion. (Anna's 1895 first marriage was also performed by a county clerk). Or perhaps, given the painful deaths that had left each of them unmarried, the couple decided to both save money and avoid attention by quietly wedding in an out-of-the-way spot.

56. Southwest Kansas Genealogical Association, *The Treesearcher* (Vols. 18-20), p. 34. Goodland is also used by novelist T.D. Shields as the site of America's new capital after Washington, D.C., is destroyed by war and climate change.

A 1900 Little Rock directory lists Annie as a seamstress; her then-husband, Max Bennett, and his brother Ike came to Little Rock in the 1870s and eventually opened successful businesses.[57] But Max, suffering from TB, brought his family to Denver in 1904. He finally died there in 1907.[58]

Anna Bennett came to America from the Austro-Hungarian Empire. At the time that she marries Louis, she already has four young children: Ida, age 12, followed by Felix (known as "Phil"), age 8; Edward (around 5); and Rosie, 3. Rose Millenson recalls Meyer inviting Louis's grown son Matt to Denver after a job he held as an architect in New York City vanished during an economic downturn. Matt will variously live with his uncle, his dad, and on his own.

Back in Philadelphia, the first Anna/Hannah Millenson lists her status in the 1910 Census as "widowed" rather than "divorced."[59]

In the years that follow, Louis' and Meyer's families continue to expand. Meyer and Theresa have another daughter, Beatrice ("Bea"), named for Baruch, on August 21, 1911. Meyer has started his own business and is now the proprietor of White Rose Hand Laundry. Meanwhile, Louis and Annie have a son on December 1, 1911. He's named Byron, also in memory of Baruch. (Somewhat oddly, both the boy and girl have "Baruch" as their Hebrew names.)

Louis continues to make cigars. Local manufacturers have sprung up throughout Colorado, with tobacco brought in by rail from wholesalers in Chicago, Baltimore, and Philadelphia. An average cigar maker, rolling 200 cigars a day, could make around $17 a week (good wages) and an experienced, faster one could earn double that.[60] Anna/Annie is a grocer, with a store in North Denver.

57. Max Bennett's brother, Ike, was married to Annie's sister Sarah, and their descendants continued to run a store in Little Rock that traced its origins back to the brothers' original businesses. It closed in 2018 after nearly 150 years.

58. Sources are online histories, family stories, and "Max Bennett Dead: Former Little Rock Man Passes Away in Denver, Col." *Daily Arkansas Gazette* (Little Rock). September 16, 1907. p. 5. Max was born in 1870 in Poland, and he and Annie married in 1894.

59. Since by this time Anna/Hannah has been given a secular divorce by Louis, presumably she also received a religious divorce, a "*get*," allowing her to remarry. But perhaps Louis had not provided a *get*, a common problem, so she called herself a widow to get around that. Or perhaps she just began calling herself a widow.

60. "Cigar Making in Colorado." *Colorado Encyclopedia (Online)*. Accessed at: http://bit.ly/36k3PX2

As for Jacob, his retail career takes a puzzling turn. A Washington, D.C., directory from 1911 indicates he's opened a Regal Shoe Store; the listing continues until at least 1913. Regal boasted in its ads that Napoleon, Czar Nicholas II, and the Emperor of China all wore its popularly priced brand of high-end shoes. Regal is apparently unfazed by details like the fact that Napoleon died in 1821 and the company was founded in 1893.

A little digging raises some questions. To begin with, display ads for Regal Shoes before and during Jacob's time in Washington show a different address than his business address in the directory. Was he a wholesaler? Meanwhile, sons George and Lester are living at the same D.C. residence as Jacob (the youngest sibling, Irving, is still in school), but they're working as "clerks" at an unspecified location. Were they with Jacob? Moreover, Lester is shown as the catcher for both halves of a doubleheader played by the East New Market baseball team on July 4, 1912, muddling residency even more.

A family story says that Rebecca suffered a stroke around 1908 and was in a wheelchair, causing Lester to drop out of middle school in order to help his mother and the family business. George, meanwhile, had been at a college prep high school in Baltimore. The time in Washington might have been related to Rebecca seeing doctors there. It might have been a simple case of the older boys wanting a more robust social life than rural Maryland could offer. Or there might have been a connection to the economic health of the East New Market store at the time.

With Rebecca sidelined and running up medical bills, an extra line of business could have been important. One of Jacob's granddaughters, Leslie Millenson Leibowitz, remembers Belle Beneman, Rebecca's sister, telling her, "You remind me of Rebecca—she was the brains of the family." Belle also characterized Jacob as a "ne'er do well" who "would bet on two flies climbing up the wall."

Whatever the veracity of those impressions—and Jacob clearly fared better when he followed the Benemans rather than his older brother—East New Market may have been struggling to remain a center of local commerce. With the automobile transforming the American economy, the importance of a town's proximity to rail and water transport, much less being a short walk or horseback ride for local residents, was waning.

In 1900, U.S. states registered 8,000 automobiles. By 1914, when an automobile Jacob was driving was involved in a severe accident, the U.S. had 1.8 million registered cars and trucks, with that total jumping by 50 percent every year. Fortunately, no one was hurt in Jacob's accident, according to a local newspaper account. A separate Baltimore newspaper article listing new automobile licenses shows that Jacob's vehicle was a Buick Touring Car purchased just four months previously, its Cadillac-style electric starter and powerful headlights enabling the Buick to command a price roughly two and half times that of the more modestly equipped Ford Model T.

But Jacob's prosperity was endangered within just a few months by another store fire. In this case he actually appears to have been underinsured. Here's my summary of an item that appeared in a local newspaper on December 6, 1914:

> "The worst conflagration ever known in the history of the town" began shortly before 7 o'clock in the J. Millenson & Son store and then swept through the town, with losses estimated at $35,000. The J. Millenson & Son dry goods store, with clothing and dresses and a large general line, as well as dry goods, is estimated to have had losses between $9,000 and $10,000, having just received a $2,000 shipment of goods, with insurance of between $6,500 and $7,500.[61]

61. "Big Conflagration at East New Market." *Cambridge Chronicle*. Dec. 6, 1914. Accessed at: http://www.collinsfactor.com/newspaper/news1900.htm

Fortunately, while Jacob owned the contents of the store, he did not own the store building. Millenson's Department Store was rebuilt as a two-story structure on a corner in the main intersection of town. Today, the location is home to the fire department and has a plaque identifying it as a historic site.[62]

In Denver, meanwhile, Meyer and Theresa have another daughter, Rebecca ("Beck"), on June 4, 1913. Helen, their final child, is born on April 20, 1917.

TRAGEDY BREAKS UP A FAMILY

Louis's family in Denver is a large one: Louis and Annie, her four kids, and the one they had together. Meyer, prospering, helps his brother financially, according to a later family recollection.

But on April 11, 1915, tragedy strikes. Annie suddenly dies at age 40, leaving five children and a stack of unpaid medical bills. Grieving, Louis is also handed the job of estate administrator.[63]

Before the summer is out, the probate court approves an expenditure of $250 from the estate's funds to buy one-way railroad tickets for the four Bennett children to New York to live with an aunt and uncle they've never met. The money also covers "suitable wearing apparel and such other things as may be necessary" and is to be reimbursed later to the estate. The two boys get new suits and caps for $4.75 each; there's no record of the girls getting anything.

Image: Undated photo thought to be Annie Bennett.

Source: Ann Pineles

62. The description from the state historical trust puts the year at "about" 1913. In fact, it must have been 1915 or afterwards. Department of Planning. Maryland Historical Trust. "Old Millenson's Department Store. D-662." Accessed at: https://mht.maryland.gov/secure/medusa/PDF/Dorchester/D-662.pdf

63. Annie's probate dragged on through the end of 1924.

The four children do not end up living together with relatives, but that's a separate story. The estate's loan is eventually paid back in a check sent by Ida Bennett, the first of the children to reach age 21, on February 23, 1918.

The court record lays out just a few bare facts. Annie's medical treatment for an unspecified purpose began on March 15 and continued until she died a little less than a month later. What happened? In researching this genealogy, I was able to fill in a large missing piece of the puzzle by reaching Annie Bennett's granddaughter, Ann Janowitz Pineles, the only child of Annie Bennett's oldest daughter, Ida. (Ida later called herself by the more Americanized first name, "Edith.") I happened to talk to Ann Pineles, named after her late grandmother, on her 90th birthday. I asked what she knew about the circumstances of her namesake's death.

Annie Bennett Millenson "died of blood poisoning," said Pineles, or what we would now call sepsis. "She had an abortion."

Before going any further, let's step back for a moment and try to imagine the family situation at this terrible time.

Louis has been married for six years to his new wife and, by all appearances, has gotten a fresh start in life. With five kids, money is tight. Still, while Annie runs the grocery store, Louis has a steady job at a cigar company in which his wife (perhaps from her first husband) has an ownership stake, probate records later show. With Meyer's family and one of Louis's grown sons also in Denver, there's a lot of family time.

"Uncle Louis was a big sport" with an "engaging" personality, Meyer's daughter Libby will later recall. "He was always a leader of doing this, going there, doing that." Also, said Libby, "He was a big gambler"—a description that echoes Belle Beneman's description of Jacob.

All in all, things are going well – until, in an unspeakably awful way, everything falls apart.

What emotional turmoil did the decision to have an abortion cause Annie and Louis?

What about its gut-wrenching aftermath, a shocking death followed by Louis feeling compelled to send away four young children who have come to see him as their father? What does Louis's son Matt think of all this in light of Louis's previous abandonment history? (Matt will get divorced from his wife, Esther, later that same year and their son, Lester, will eventually take the last name of his stepfather, Greenfield. In early 1920, Matt will marry Rose, who is seven years younger than he is.)

What about the impact of Annie's death on Meyer's family? Meyer's wife, Theresa, is just three years older than her sister-in-law. She and Annie are both immigrants, both in a second marriage, and in 1911 they even have overlapping pregnancies. Theresa gives birth to a girl and Annie to a boy, but both children are named after the same grandparent. What is the impact of Annie's death on Theresa?

Perhaps most importantly, what is the effect of Annie's death on her four children, who in just a few years have seen both birth parents die and then been sent away by their stepfather? When I asked Ann Pineles what her mother, age 15 at the time of Annie's death, said about Louis, Ann replied, "She never talked about him."

As for that long and lonely train ride across the country by the Bennett siblings, Ann told me: "They never spoke about it."

(My grandfather, Joe, never talked about Louis either.)

Sometime after Annie's death, Louis leaves the painful memories of Denver behind and travels with his young son Byron to live with Jacob. We know this because of another letter in a newspaper.

On October 28, 1915, an open letter appears in *Der Deutsche Correspondent* endorsing the Democratic candidate for governor, Emerson Columbus Harrington. The signatories, writing as "we Germans" who live in Dorchester County, proclaim that as "citizens and neighbors" of Harrington, they can attest to his "upright character."[64] Among the signatories are "J. Millenson" and "Lou Millenson."

64. *Der Deutsche Correspondent*. October 28, 1915, p. 8. Accessed at: http://bit.ly/2twQf4H

65. Ada Millenson thought of Paul Weiner as a real brother. He died on December 31, 1988.

By the time that letter appears, however, Louis has returned to Baltimore.

AN UNSTABLE STABILITY

Jewish law, codified at a time when being a single parent was a genuine hardship, prescribes just a 30-day mourning period for a spouse, in contrast with the one-year mourning period for a parent. Six months after Annie's death, on October 23, 1915, Louis marries Mary (Miriam) Gardner, an Eastern European-born divorcee with a 14-year-old son, Paul Weiner, from Mary's previous marriage to Jacob Weiner.[65]

Annie Bennett's maiden name was also Weiner. The name is not uncommon, and Annie's obituary lists only sisters. But it's possible Mary's ex-husband was a cousin of Annie's, and she knew Louis previously. It could also be either coincidence or a clue to a Millenson connection that Paul's middle name was Nathan. Another possible connection comes from the 1910 Census, which shows Mary living with her mother and son on Exeter Street, not far from Baruch and Dena's home.

Image: Undated photo thought to be Louis Millenson.

Source: Howard Dobres

On March 30, 1917, Louis and Mary have a son of their own, David. He has severe mental disabilities and is sent at a young age to Rosewood State Training School. A daughter, Ada, is born on November 24, 1918.[66] Louis and family live with Dena in Baruch and Dena's house; in January 1917, Dena formally transfers ownership to Louis. Mary runs a dry goods store, and Dena helps raise the younger children.

66. A 1953 newspaper article discusses Ada, then known as Ada Dobres, helping the ladies' auxiliary of the Bobroisker Lodge, a Jewish group, put on entertainment for the 400 children at Rosewood. The facility was closed in 2009.

Image: Undated photo thought be Mary Millenson with Ada and possibly David or Byron.

Source: Howard Dobres

The cigar industry is fading fast. After World War I, handmade cigars rapidly lose out in popularity to less expensive, machine-made cigarettes, particularly among women. Louis gives it another go as a cigar retailer, but it's in vain. In March 1922, he sells the contents of a store at 102 North Potomac Street (candy, cigars, store fixtures, and accumulated "goodwill") for $42.[67]

67. A brief notice in the July 8, 1921, *Baltimore Daily Record* mentions a "chattel agreement" (essentially, a rental) involving Louis and the Baltimore Soda Fountain Manufacturing Co. This diversification wasn't enough to save the business, located separately from the dry goods store.

Ada will later recall her childhood as a spartan existence. The home was heated by a wood-burning stove in the kitchen, and the toilet was an outhouse. Things were not much better even in 1946, when Rose Millenson visited on a hot summer day. By then Mary was suffering from serious health issues, and Louis was losing his eyesight. Rose recalls him sitting on a chair in the kitchen, and "the flies were eating him alive." She screamed at Ada, then still living at home. "I said, 'Listen. Matt is sending money every single month, Joe is sending money every single month, Sam is sending money. And you tell me you can't put a screen door on?'"

Ada's sons and my father, meanwhile, remembered one other feature of the house: a carved-wood cigar store Indian that Louis somehow brought home.[68]

In Denver, Meyer was also running a store, albeit a far larger enterprise than that of either of his two brothers. It was called Western Beef Company. We don't know what meat-cutting skills Meyer picked up from his dad—in their book on Baltimore Jews, Goldstein and Weiner write of empty yards in the packed Jewish neighborhood being used to slaughter chickens. However, Meyer's time with Otto Shatz had certainly shown him that selling meat could generate a lot of cash.[69]

Daughter Libby later recalled that Meyer started Western Beef in the wake of a work accident. While driving the wagon for his laundry business, Meyer's horse bolted and his leg was severely injured, leaving him with a running sore for years. Meyer wouldn't let the doctor amputate, but he did sell the laundry and opened a grocery business. The incident occurred not long after Nate was born.

Libby also recalled Meyer as a "great mixer" who enjoyed all sorts of people—Blacks, Polish, Spanish, and the men who worked in the mines—and would bring people back to the house. He spoke German in addition to Yiddish, and in Denver he learned Spanish.

68. In an era when much of the population was illiterate, storeowners used various figurines to represent their trade. Since Indians had introduced the settlers to tobacco, that was the representation chosen by those who sold tobacco products. For more, see Wikipedia at: http://bit.ly/2uS5XYY

69. In a 1911 report by the Colorado Bureau of Labor Statistics, Otto Shatz Grocery is listed as having 18 male and 4 female employees. Shatz, meanwhile, had his eye on even greater riches, as his 1904 prospectus for the Otto Shatz Mining, Leasing & Developing Company illustrates.

Meyer's inclusiveness is particularly noteworthy because it came during a largely forgotten period of Colorado history when the Ku Klux Klan constituted a powerful presence. By the mid-1920s, Denver's mayor, governor, and many other Colorado officials were KKK members.[70]

Western Beef prospered. The 1920 Census shows that Meyer's family employed a 65-year-old widow as live-in help. Later, Libby and Bea would remember a comfortable life that included riding lessons, Sunday dinner outings, and the kids being allowed to buy penny candy.

As a teenager, Nate hosted social gatherings of a Jewish youth group called "the OWL Club"[71] and attended birthday parties where "the evening was spent in dancing and games."[72] However, sister Libby recalled enough troubling behavior that her parents eventually sent Nate off to a military academy for high school. An internet search found that he was enrolled for at least the 1923–24 school year at Wentworth Military Academy in rural Lexington, Missouri, a school that pledged "to produce men of culture, ability and character."

Meanwhile, in East New Market, Jacob and Rebecca sell the entire inventory in their store in 1917 to the Philadelphia Underselling Co.[73] They move to Cumberland, a transportation and industrial hub in the mountains of Western Maryland.

The Benemans have already started a clothing store there, and Jacob and Rebecca's oldest son, George, has opened Millenson Piano Company. Irving ("Babe") briefly puts his pharmacy training to use by founding the Cumberland Drug and Extract Co., but he soon goes into business with brother Lester running a loan company. Rebecca dies on October 2, 1921, just 56 years old. The family gets another scare a few years later when, at a local hotel, the steel cable holding an elevator in which Jacob and two other men are riding snaps. The cage falls, but the men fortunately escape injury.

70. Goodstein, Phil H. *In The Shadow of the Klan: When the KKK Ruled Denver 1920-1926*. New Social Publications, 2006

71. *Denver Jewish News.* January 11, 1922

72. *Denver Jewish News.* December 28, 1921

73. East New Market Items. *The Daily Banner* (Cambridge, Maryland.) August 16, 1917

The story of the First Millensons might now be starting to draw to a quiet conclusion. By the end of 1926:

- Louis has turned 62 years old and has settled in with his young family in Baltimore. His older children (Matt, Joe, and Sam) live with their own families in Denver, Washington, and Philadelphia, respectively.

- Jacob retired in 1923, running a "going out of business sale" for his Regal shoe store in Cumberland, also known as J. Millenson and Son, in December of that year. At year's end 1926, he is 60. Since coming to Cumberland, Jacob and his sons have run a variety of businesses separately or in various combinations.

- Meyer, a decade younger, is still working full time in Denver. His oldest child, Nate, got married on December 8, 1925. Meyer and Theresa are surely looking forward to future weddings for their four girls.

A peaceful close. Except that on January 1, 1927, the story of Meyer Millenson and family takes a dramatic and unexpected turn.

A SHOCKING DEATH

Meyer Sussman, interviewed a few months before his 80th birthday, said he was an upperclassman at Denver University when he discovered the truth about his namesake's death. Meyer Millenson committed suicide.

That revelation didn't come from Bea Millenson Sussman, Meyer's mother, but from a cousin, a daughter of Libby Millenson Koplin. As for the "why," the family spoke vaguely of "financial reasons" even decades later.

My dad had lived with his Uncle Matt and Aunt Rose for a while after returning from World War II. In his telling, Meyer's family had once owned a substantial amount of real estate in downtown Denver, but they had to sell it after Meyer "put his head in the oven."

Image: A studio photo of the Meyer Millenson family from around 1919.

Front row: Helen, Rebecca (Beck)

Middle row: Meyer and Theresa

Back row: Beatrice (Bea), Nathan (Nate) and Libby

Source: Meyer and Harry Sussman

That's all I knew in 1978 when, traveling across the country by bus, I visited Nate Millenson in Tucson, where he was living with his third wife, Amparo Gallegos Millenson, and his 12-year-old stepdaughter, April. Nate was hospitable and expansive. He told me his father committed suicide because of losses suffered in the stock market crash. He also complained that he was unfairly cast as the "black sheep" of the family.

But when I spoke to Nate's sister Libby, also local, she told a very different story. Meyer, she said, had committed suicide because of Nate's gambling debts. Rose Millenson confirmed that account. Meyer, she said, "was a very lovely man" who "couldn't take what his son did to him," including forging his father's signature on checks to pay gambling debts.

Years later, Libby, being interviewed by one of her grandchildren, added that

> Meyer went to his banker, and the banker wanted a blanket mortgage on all his property. And he gave him [the banker] that blanket mortgage. That night, he committed suicide, depressed that he'd signed all his land away.

Whatever caused Meyer to take his own life—and it's important to remember that clinical depression was little understood at that time—this tragedy and the events that followed were not in any way private.

The stock market first crashed on October 24, 1929. Meyer committed suicide on January 1, 1927. On January 2, a five-column, all-caps headline in *The Denver Post* proclaimed, "Widely Known Denverite Rents Room and Ends Life with Gas." A short column of type on the left, with the bare facts, sits next to an enormous family photo of Meyer, Theresa, and their children.

The article tells of the "widely known Denver meat dealer" disappearing from his home early Friday morning, December 31. His body was found Saturday evening, January 1, in the gas-filled kitchenette of an apartment "which he had rented for the evident purpose of ending his life." A neighbor smelled gas and investigated. The article continued:

> Millenson, married and father of five children, had draped a blanket over his head and shoulders in the shape of a hood, leaned over the gas plate and opened all three burners.
>
> Mental derangement induced by worry over financial reverses is believed to have prompted his act . . . .
>
> [Millenson] appeared at the rooming house Friday morning, paid his room rent a week in advance, joked with the landlady and was not seen again until his body was found.

> Deputy Coroner William O'Brien said he believed the man had been dead possibly fourteen hours.
>
> Millenson's pockets contained a number of letters in Hebrew.

Meyer was buried at Mt. Nebo Memorial Park in Aurora, Colorado, the same cemetery as Anna Bennett Millenson and her first husband, Max. Under Jewish law, suicide would disqualify him from burial there, but the tradition often finds quiet ways around difficulties. This may explain why the *Denver Jewish News* did not mention Meyer's death.

Meyer's headstone contains just three lines, all in English: "Meyer Millenson. 1876-1927. Here Rests a Woodman of the World." In the upper left corner is the symbol of the Woodmen of the World, a fraternal organization that also provided life insurance to its members. In the upper right corner is the Jewish symbol of a seven-branched menorah.

The newspaper's reference to him having "a number of letters in Hebrew" undoubtedly refers to notes written in Yiddish to his family, but we don't know their contents.

What we do know is that Meyer's substantial estate, with an initial estimated worth of $45,000, became part of a protracted probate court battle involving creditors. We also know that Theresa filed a lawsuit to compel payment of a commercial life insurance policy, although we do not know the outcome. And we know that Nate's problems with gambling and other questionable activities surfaced in subsequent newspaper accounts. Meanwhile, financial issues eventually forced Meyer's family to move out of the two-story, double house at 1075 – 85 Clarkson Street they bought in 1921 for $10,000.

Theresa, say family members, never spoke about any of this.

Image: The Jewish cemetery in Grinkishok in 2018.

Source: Jonathan Feinberg

PART THREE

What Was Built, What Was Left Behind

The First American Millensons

CHAPTER EIGHT

We know next to nothing about the lives the Millensons lived in Europe. We don't know the impact of anti-Semitism, poverty, and famine or what it was like moving from country to country while trying to keep the family intact and survive. Nate Millenson was right when he declared, "The Millensons aren't too communicative. Never were."

What we do know is that in America the First Millensons followed in the footsteps of so many other immigrants who came here with little education or money: they did what they had to do. They worked in factories (slaughtering meat, rolling cigars) or started a store (dry goods, a department store, a laundry, a meat market). Whatever the family's disagreements or differing circumstances, however, all the evidence we have suggests they continued to care deeply about each other.[74]

74. For instance, the June 14, 1920, *Cumberland Evening Times* recorded that "Myer Millenson" had traveled all the way from Denver to visit his brother, "J. Millenson." Presumably, he also stopped in Baltimore to see Louis, although the big-city papers would not have noted it.

AMERICANIZING

You could judge how successfully the Millensons Americanized by looking at their children's economic or educational achievements. Or you could use a different yardstick, one invoking the family's passion for a game that was rapidly emerging as "America's National Pastime," baseball.

Jacob's son Lester was a catcher for the East New Market team. Irving played shortstop. Both thought they might go "pro," and Lester even tried out for the New York Yankees (presumably a farm team). Later, Lester and Irving—who, with the nickname of "Babe," married a woman named "Ruth"—would help bring a higher-level, minor league baseball team to Cumberland.

Among Louis's kids, Sam was talented enough as a catcher to try out for the Philadelphia Athletics. Years later, Sam would show his grandchildren the gnarled fingers he'd earned from foul tips and other abuse behind the plate. Joe would play catch with my dad when I was young and Joe was in his mid-70s. I remember them using well-worn, flat leather gloves and a long-ago-turned-brown baseball Joe had snagged as a foul ball at some game.

Among the younger of Louis's children, Byron was also a baseball enthusiast. And Ada remembered being taken to baseball games by her father as a little girl and being told by her mom, Mary, to make sure her dad—whom his grandkids eventually called by the Yiddish term Zayde—didn't lose his straw hat. That sweet picture is balanced, however, by Ada's memory of Louis as a man tough on his wives and tough on his children. His other children certainly would have agreed.

Meanwhile, Meyer's daughter Bea Millenson Sussman and her husband, "Tex" Sussman, helped found a boys baseball league in Colorado. Sisters Libby Millenson Koplin and "Beck" Millenson Meselson were also avid baseball fans.

Over time even tight-knit immigrant families inevitably assimilate into the larger culture. A 1905 study of "Russian" Jewish immigrants opined, and not in a negative way, that Americanization tended "to make the young Jewish man more of a social being . . . more easily sharing the faults and virtues of German, American and Irish young men."[75]

It's no surprise that Millenson family ties loosened or disappeared over time, particularly as the post-World War II years brought even greater geographical dispersion. But it's also important to remember that the stories revealed here highlight the extent to which those ties were likely strained by the ways in which the children of Louis, Jacob, and Meyer grew up with very different life experiences.

75. *The Russian Jew in the United States: Studies of Social Conditions in New York, Philadelphia and Chicago, with a Description of Rural Settlements.* Charles Seligman Bernheimer, editor. Philadelphia: John C. Winston Company, 1905

When Irving was 14, for example, he won a dollar in a writing contest sponsored by *The Sun* by describing how his pet bantam hen in rural East New Market tried to protect its chicks. In contrast, when his cousin Matt was that age, he and his siblings, going hungry in a cramped Philadelphia apartment, were writing a desperate plea in a Yiddish newspaper because his abandoned mother couldn't provide similar protection. And when their cousin Becca was roughly 14, her father committed suicide, an event that not only brought an agonizing end to a comfortable life, but was splashed all over the Denver newspapers for everyone to see.

For all that, we have to be careful about assumptions regarding family relationships. Take the case of the four Bennett children sent away by Louis in 1915. In 1978, Meyer's daughter Libby knew the name of Ida/Edith's daughter, Ann Janowitz. And Ann, when I contacted her in 2020, told me she'd stayed in touch for years with Byron and Ada. Yet neither Byron's daughters nor Ada's sons knew anything about those contacts!

When it came to religion, Baruch's boys, like so many other children of Jewish immigrants, drifted (or perhaps ran) from their parents' observance. Along with the allure of secular American society, the boys' memories of the harsh teaching methods of Eastern European *cheders*—teachers routinely beat or whipped recalcitrant students—could have played a role. At home Baruch likely embraced that same stern approach. Louis, Jacob, and Meyer knew exactly what they were rejecting. As Libby Millenson Koplin told me, "That's why they left home. They didn't want to be that religious."

Meyer was nominally Reform and, like many Jews, regularly attended temple as much for social as religious reasons. As for Jacob and his family on Maryland's Eastern Shore, it's unclear where the nearest Jewish place of worship would have been, although the family did affiliate with a Reform congregation in Cumberland. Louis, who spent most

Image: The Bennett children sent away by Louis Millenson in 1915 quietly stayed in touch with their half-brother, Byron. This photo from a Bennett family event around 1955 shows Byron, in glasses, standing in the second row on the left.

Sitting in front of him are, from the left, Rose Bennett Endlich and Edith (Ida) Bennett Janowitz (his half-sisters); wife, Esther Millenson; Eli Dublin (a Bennett uncle); and Ethel Bennett and her husband, Phil Bennett, Byron's half-brother. Half-brother Ed Bennett is standing upper right next to Jack Pineles and wife, Ann Janowitz Pineles.

Source: Ann Janowitz Pineles.

of his life on the East Coast, seems to have affiliated with Orthodox or Conservative synagogues, and his gravestone is the only traditional Jewish one. However, his personal degree of observance, as we've seen, remains a giant question mark.

We know very little about the lives of the Millenson men's wives. All we can say is that they too pitched in to help earn a living, working as seamstresses or running a store, as well as persevering through family moves to different cities, losing a child, losing a spouse, and other challenges.

After Meyer's suicide on January 1, 1927, his wife, Theresa, lived another 33 years, dying at age 83 in Arizona on January 4, 1960. Her simple headstone—her name, years of birth and death, and a menorah symbol—is next to Meyer's at Mt. Nebo Memorial Park.

Just 18 months after Meyer's death, Jacob died in Cumberland. The date was June 8, 1928, a few weeks short of his 62nd birthday. He and Rebecca are buried next to each other in Cumberland's Eastview Cemetery.

Meanwhile, Louis, the brother who spent a lifetime puffing on cigars and breathing in tobacco dust, lives to age 84 (though his tombstone says 83). He dies in Baltimore on March 2, 1949, or roughly a century after Baruch's name change made him the first Millenson. Louis's first wife, Anne/Hannah, died in Philadelphia on August 3, 1933, at age 65. And though Mary was much younger than Louis, she died just eight months after him, on November 13, 1949. They share a common headstone (where his first name is spelled "Lewis") and are buried in Baltimore's Beth Jacob Cemetery.

Louis's gravestone refers to him by his English and Hebrew names: "Yitzchak Leib b"r Baruch," Isaac Louis, the son of Reb Baruch. Had there been an epitaph, it might have read: "Once a cigar maker, always a cigar maker."

Image: Tombstones of Lewis and Mary Millenson in Baltimore (top) and of Meyer Millenson in Aurora, Colorado (bottom).

Source: FindAGrave.com.

Grinkishok (Again)

CHAPTER NINE

A letter in the archives of the Yad Vashem Holocaust remembrance center begins, "On the first day of the war in Grinkiškis, June 1, 1941, I escaped on a bicycle and arrived in Russia by way of Latvia." The writer, a man named Yaakov Levi, goes on to describe how he joined the Russian Army, was wounded in battle, escaped from a German-run hospital, and then, after the war, returned to his village.

WHAT WAS LOST, WHAT REMAINS

Almost exactly three months after Levi first fled Lithuania, the Jews of Grinkiškis and neighboring villages were rounded up and taken to the town of Krakes. On September 2, 1941, they were made to dig their own graves before being shot to death by Nazi SS troops aided by local Lithuanians.

"The night before the killings my nephew escaped from Krakes to the forest with another 10 to 12 young men," writes Levi, "and they were killed by the Lithuanian partisans." Another group of Jews that included the village rabbi sought refuge in a nearby monastery. Although the nuns there told them they were going to be killed the next day, the rabbi refused pleas to try to escape, saying such an attempt would be a disaster. The next day, they were all shot.

The only survivor, writes Levi, was "a Jew by the name of Raybshtein who came out in the night from the midst of the dead bodies and hid in the forest."

Levi eventually left Europe and settled in the Israeli city of Holon. Writing in Hebrew in 2007, as an elderly man, he said he was concerned that Yad Vashem did not have an adequate list of the Jews who had once lived in Grinkiškis. So he provided the names from memory, starting with his own family ("Levi, Shmuel, about 55, proprietor of a fabric store; Levi, Miryam, daughter of Aharon, about 53, wife of the proprietor of a fabric store.") He eventually listed 120 people, including some whose presence he remembered but whose names he'd forgotten ("widower;" "sold tools in the marketplace").

Not long before the Nazis arrived, Grinkishok (the Yiddish name for Grinkiškis) was briefly a center of Jewish learning. The head of the Mir Yeshiva, which was forced by the Soviets to disperse to four different towns, quietly moved by himself to Grinkishok. But as the Nazi threat grew, Rabbi Eliezer Yehuda Finkel and many of the leaders and students of what would become one of the world's premier yeshivas managed to escape using some of the precious exit visas frantically being issued Jews by the Japanese consul-general in Lithuania.[76]

76. Blumberg, Raphael. *They Called Him Rebbe: The Life and Good Works of Rabbi Boruch Milikowsky*. New York: Urim Publications, 2007

Well before the Nazis arrived, the Jewish population of Grinkishok had been shrinking. By the early 20th century, enough Grinkishokers had come to America that the 1912 *American Jewish Year Book* lists an "Anshe Grinkeshok" burial society in New York City with 65 members. It was located in Bedford-Stuyvesant, a Brooklyn neighborhood to which Jews were moving from the overcrowded Lower East Side. A cluster of other Grinkishokers ended up in Homestead, Pennsylvania, whose famous steel mill propelled the area's prosperity.

With some persistent Googling, I also ferreted out names of one-time Grinkishok residents such as Israel B. Brodie, an early American Zionist and industrialist who worked closely with Justice Louis D. Brandeis; Joseph Selig Glick, another prominent Zionist and the publisher of the first Yiddish newspaper in Pittsburgh; Nathan Friedlander, one of the first Jewish settlers in Alabama; and Nat Bregman, a man Nelson Mandela described as his "first white friend." Meanwhile, a prominent Jewish humorist of the 1920s, Jacob Richman, made Grinkishok the location of one of his fictional characters.

Abe Feinberg writes in his memoir of being told that the shul where his parents once prayed had been burned and reduced to rotting timbers. Nonetheless, some seven decades later, in July of 2018, Abe's son Dr. Jonathan Feinberg decided to visit Grinkishok and other former Lithuanian shtetls with relatives from both his mother's and father's sides of the family.

Grinkiškis remains small, with only about 700 people.[77] There are no traces of the synagogue, of course. But in a self-printed book with photos of the trip, Jonathan described the Jewish cemetery as being located on a "lush green field with a beautiful forest background." Unfortunately, the inscriptions on the few stones that remain are so faded from weather and neglect that they are mostly unreadable.

The Jews of Grinkiškis might be long gone, but anti-Semitism has lingered. A resident who said he was four years old when his father moved into a house the Jews had "left" was, wrote Jonathan in the book, "animated and jolly and told the story of how his father's friends had asked him if he had found any of the Jews' gold under the floorboards."

Still, Jonathan wrote me in an email, "Our trip to Lithuania was fantastic, and I did feel the family connection."[78]

77. A bland, eight-minute virtual driving tour of Grinkiškis, presumably for Lithuanian tourists, was posted online in 2012. It can be accessed at https://www.youtube.com/watch?v=ZVVZ0-Wd_cw

78. Jonathan Feinberg. Personal communication. August 6, 2018. Jonathan died unexpectedly of a heart attack at age 80 in the fall of 2019.

(3)

26) משפחת ברוק – 2 מבוגרים.

27) ברוק ואשתו + 4 ילדים. סנדלר.

28) קרים ואשתו. בעל מאפיה.

29) ליפשיץ – 2.

30) ליפשיץ – 4.

שמות משפחה לא זכורים :

2 – חנות מכולת.

3 – חנות סידקית.

1 – אלמן.

3 – חנות מכולת.

4 – מכרו כלים בשווקים.

6 – רוכלים.

<u>סה"כ 120</u>

האנשים המפורטים מוכרים
הם גרו בעיירה גרינקישק
והם כולם הושמדו.

לוי יעקב

Image: The last page of a 2007 letter to Yad Vashem by Yaakov Levi, a former Grinkiškis resident. The handwritten postscript reads, "The [120] people who are listed here are known to have lived in the village of Grinkiškis, and they all were slaughtered," followed by a signature.

Source: Yad Vashem

AFTERWORD

My father, Roy Handen Millenson, died on April 9, 2017, one day before the first night of Passover. Although dementia had been steadily eroding his mind for years, his death at age 95 nonetheless forced me to confront the uncomfortably obvious: our lives and memories are fragile, and what seems indelibly imprinted today will soon enough be erased unless we act to prevent it.

I have always loved history. Digging into my father's personal history in order to assemble a small memory book for the shiva period inevitably led to wider internet surfing to try to uncover the Millenson past. Slowly, the lives of those who had just been a dry list of names started to come alive.

My dabbling didn't devolve into sustained research, however, until a surprise email and attached letter arrived on March 27, 2019, from a woman named Rachel L. Eisenhauer. It announced, "I'm more than likely your 2nd cousin."

The Eisenhauers were a German-Catholic family from Baltimore with no "history of any Jewish relations," wrote Rachel. No history, that is, until a DNA test in November 2015 unexpectedly revealed a surprise. After a "three-and-a-half-year journey to clear up a mystery that we didn't know existed," Rachel continued, she had come to a conclusion: "My grandfather's biological father was more than likely Louis Millenson."

Although I did not have my personal DNA information online, I did have a significant internet presence. When other Millensons whose DNA seemed to be similar had not responded to Rachel's emails, she wrote me. I immediately wrote back. That's when this seeking out the stories and secrets of the family's past began to get serious.

Rachel, who lives in Annapolis, had been regularly searching the Maryland and Colorado state archives with the methodical determination of the trained lawyer that she is. The documents she found were frequently eye-opening: birth and death certificates, lawsuits, probate court records, and even a will from Baruch's wife, Dena, filed under the name "Annie Millison." Rachel was also systematically mining information on Ancestry.com.

Leveraging our strengths, we began to assemble the Millenson story. I could provide the religious and family context. Also, although I'm not a lawyer, I am both a researcher and a former journalist with experience in investigative reporting.

As Rachel continued to add pieces to the puzzle, I cast a wide net for sources of social and economic context, such as Patricia Cooper's book *Once a Cigar Maker*, that might imbue our limited facts with meaning. We also redoubled our efforts to find contemporaneous information, including material from the American Jewish Archives, Cook County (where Chicago is located), the Colorado State Archives, the Denver Public Library, the Hebrew Union College Archives, the Historical Society of Dauphin County (Pennsylvania) and the Jewish Museum of Maryland. And I too began mining Ancestry.com as well as online archives of old newspaper stories, searching for nuggets of information.

Separately, I reached out both to relatives I knew and those I did not to see if they had any documents, photos, or family stories they might share. The biggest payoff came from a call to a Denver company listed as being run by Meyer Millenson's nearly 80-year-old grandson, Meyer Sussman. Meyer called me back shortly after I left a message, and he quickly connected me to his son, Jeff, who was already interested in family history. Jeff knew where to find stories from relatives who had been interviewed years earlier, and he even had some himself.

I in turn unearthed notes from 1978 when I interviewed Meyer Millenson's son Nate and daughter Libby on a stopover in Tucson during a cross-country bus trip. I also found a tape of an interview I did in 1988 with Rose Millenson, conducted when she was visiting in Chicago. Still, I found myself constantly regretting unasked questions. Even in 1991, when I interviewed my father and mother extensively, I simply presumed my dad didn't know much about his grandfather or other Millensons of the immigrant generation because he'd never said anything more than a few sentences about them.

In reality, however, Louis Millenson lived less than two hours away from where my dad grew up, and Louis died when my father was 27 years old—not exactly a child. Also, my father's mother and father were second cousins. In retrospect there must have been quite a few family stories my father deliberately did not share. One example: only now, looking closely at the photo album my dad inherited from his mother, do I realize there are baby pictures of him with both of his grandmothers, but there's not one photo with Grandpa Louis.

Whenever possible I've tried to crosscheck all information, since even official documents or what's literally carved on a gravestone can be inaccurate. If spellings or dates cannot be determined, I've tried to indicate that. (See Appendix D: Timeline.) However, particularly with spellings there are sometimes just too many variations to list them all. The extensive use of footnotes is meant to aid others who might wish to use this book as a foundation for further exploration. Subsequent research could delve into areas skimmed over here (e.g., various real estate transactions), correct inadvertent inaccuracies, and help answer open questions, of which there are many.

There are few individuals still alive who personally knew Louis, Jacob, or Meyer Millenson or their wives and only a handful more who even knew their children. Still, I tried to tread carefully with what I wrote. Individuals' personalities are shaped by nature and nurture alike, and the early Millensons spent years having to survive in some very harsh circumstances. While today we might wince at some of their professional and personal behaviors, the times were very different, and retrospective judgments can be all-too-easy to make from the comfort of our present-day circumstances. That same caution applies to Louis, Jacob, and Meyer's children, whom some of us knew as parents or grandparents.

All of us are in part the sum of the generations that went before. What traits did the First Millensons pass on to their descendants? While there is no definitive answer, I'd suggest that Louis deliberately voting the opposite way from what his boss ordered, and no doubt boasting about it to family and friends, signifies a strong (perhaps even "stubborn") streak of independent thinking and willingness to speak up that continues to characterize the Millenson family.

In the end, this history is meant both as a resource for others with similar genealogical interests and as a legacy to all Millenson descendants. Some fascinating findings from Emory University speak to that latter purpose. The researchers found that when children know their family history, including the uncomfortable incidents and setbacks, they develop a sense of belonging that provides a resilience lacking in peers without that tie to the past. Coherent family narratives led to measurably better self-esteem, higher levels of social competence, and less anxiety.[79]

While that's a tall order for any tale, I nonetheless hope this book provides the impetus to share the stories found here and others yet to be written with the next generation and the generations that follow.

79. Clark, Carol. "How family stories help children weather hard times." *eScience Commons*, Emory News Center. April 29, 2020. Accessed at: http://bit.ly/35vhAon

ACKNOWLEDGMENTS

I'd like to first acknowledge once again Rachel Eisenhauer and Jeff Sussman for their invaluable help on this genealogical journey. I also want to thank my siblings, Janet and Elliott, for their continual encouragement.

The sections on Lithuania benefited from what was learned on the trip to Grinkishok by Rabbi Abraham Feinberg's son Jonathan Feinberg. His sudden death was a huge loss, and I am grateful that Jon's widow, Adella Harris, gracefully continued to respond to my questions. Tragically, Adella died just before this work was completed, as did Howard Dobres, Ada's middle son, who contributed his memories of family history.

My nephew Benjamin Feinberg-Gerner (no relation to the other Feinbergs) examined Abe's papers at the American Jewish Archives. The Lithuanian Jewish history scholar Dovid Katz will forever have my gratitude for homing in on the likely derivation of the name "Millenson." Milena Zeidler, an Oxford researcher, helped link the Lithuanian famine to the possible gradual migration of Baruch and his family in a manner that included East Prussia, while U.S. researcher Bruce Bazelon helped definitively link Baruch to Harrisburg.

Individuals with ties to Grinkishokers who responded to my queries included Adina Bregman, Lori Grinker, Matthew and Ken Jacobson, and Tammy Hepps, the talented researcher and storyteller who runs the Homestead Hebrews website. Meanwhile, the deep research done by Marsha Steinberg in tracing her branch of the Abramson family tree provided persuasive evidence that it grew out of the same roots as those of Baruch and Tsvi. Digging much deeper into the family's history in Europe will require a professional genealogist.

Rabbi Levi Druk of Chabad of Downtown Baltimore unlocked the mystery of the name "Anshe Neizen" and also helped me understand the relationship between Hasidic and non-Hasidic communities in Lithuania. Rabbi Vernon Kurtz, long-time rabbi of North Suburban Synagogue Beth El (my shul), helped me decipher Baruch's tombstone, while fellow congregant Frank Stern was kind enough to translate *Der Deutsche Correspondent*'s German into English. Harvard scholar Caroline Light went well beyond the call of duty in retrieving her notes on the heartbreaking correspondence in Yiddish between Louie Millenson and his children and in directing me to an archive with microfilm of the original source. Dovid Katz once again came through by referring me to an ace Yiddish translator living in Israel, J. Felendler.

In addition to thanking Wayne Burton and Howard Wolinsky for their encouragement to pursue Jewish genealogy, I also want to thank others whose assistance helped make this possible. They came from all branches of the family, from individuals I already knew, and individuals I had no idea existed. Bringing everyone together for this project was a joy and a privilege.

Those connected to the Louis side of the family, through blood ties or otherwise, include Carol and Howard (z"l) Dobres, Sheldon and Sandy Dobres, Michael Dobres, David Goldstein, Jay Kaufman, Debra Millenson Kroneberger, Sheree Kaufman Meyer, Jeff Millenson, Leslie Millenson, Michael M. Millenson, Ann Millenson Mishner, and Ann Janowitz Pineles.

Those connected to the Jacob side of the family, through blood ties or otherwise, include George Beneman II, Otto Diaz, Robert Millenson, Leslie Millenson Leibowitz, Gaby Leibowitz, John Lowenberg, Mark Lowenberg, Paul Lowenberg, and Nancy Weller.

Image: A studio photo of the Roy Millenson family from around 1976.

Front row: Roy, Charlotte and Elliott

Back row: Janet and Michael

Source: Michael L. Millenson

Those connected to the Meyer side of the family, through blood ties or otherwise, include Joe Feldman, Andy Meselson, Diane Schoen, Harry Sussman, and Meyer Sussman.

Finally, a big thank you to my daughter, Alissa, for her invaluable design work in turning this information into a beautiful book (along with a big assist from Nan and Biff Barnes and their team at Stories To Tell Books), and to Jeff Sussman and his dad, Meyer Sussman, for underwriting the production of a printed book that will be a genuine family keepsake.

ABOUT THE AUTHOR

Michael Louis Millenson was born in 1953 in Washington, D.C., the son of Roy Handen Millenson and Charlotte Katz Millenson. He was named after his mother's father (Michael Louis Katz) and his father's grandfather (Louis Millenson), and he is the middle of three siblings, between Janet Ann and Elliott Jacob Millenson. He grew up in Bethesda, Maryland, and attended college at Washington University in St. Louis. Since 1980, Michael has lived in the Chicago area, where his career as a journalist, author, consultant, and researcher has focused on working to improve health care safety, quality, and patient-centeredness. He and his wife, Susan, are the parents of Daniel Moses Millenson and Alissa Joelle Millenson.

Image: Michael, Susan, Daniel, and Alissa Millenson at a neighbor's sukkah in Highland Park, Illinois, October 11, 2020.

Source: Alissa Millenson

Appendices

APPENDIX A

THE MEANING OF THE NAME "MILLENSON"

The origin of the name "Millenson" has always been a mystery. We know Baruch Abramson's family was trying to keep him out of the czar's army by giving him a new last name that would mark him as a draft-exempt "only son." But why "Millenson"? And how could a group of inquisitive individuals like Baruch's descendants not have passed down an answer to that question?

At one time, my only-halfway tongue-in-cheek theory was that Millenson was a Swedish name. Not that Baruch's family was Swedish, of course, but Lithuania lies across the Baltic Sea from Sweden, a one-time European power. Perhaps Millenson or Millensen was the name of a swashbuckling Swedish sea captain or a well-known brand of Swedish stove. Alas, a Swedish colleague popped that bubble. Swedish names with "son" or "sen" reflect the father's first name, and "Millen" isn't a Swedish one.

However, while researching this history, I was struck by a sudden realization. As I looked at how the name was spelled on Baruch's tombstone, I realized that concentrating on "Millenson" was misleading. The Abramson family chose the name in Lithuania, and they spoke Yiddish, not English.

In Yiddish, the name came across as something like "Milenzahn" (pronounced "Mee-len-zahn"), which can be Anglicized into "Milensohn" and "Millensohn." However, I couldn't find anyone with that name or anything close to it on JewishGen. The nearest I could come to "Milensohn" was a smattering of German Lutherans (nowhere close to Grinkishok) or a small town in Galicia named "Meilen," dubious in pronunciation and geography. And the translation was still a meaningless, "Son of Millen."

Then, towards the end of 2019, I came upon the book *Lithuanian Jewish Culture*. It's a beautiful, oversized, coffee-table-type volume of history and photos written by an American scholar named Dovid Katz. Katz is a distinguished Yiddish culture expert who lives in Vilnius. The book was published (in English) by a Lithuanian press.

I found Katz's email address and sent him a note complimenting him on the book and asking whether he might have any clue as to what Millenson might mean. He couldn't offer any insights, but he referred me to a scholarly expert on Jewish names.

I thanked him and wrote back, "If Baruch's mom's name was 'Milla' instead of 'Leah,' I'd have a bull's-eye."

To which Katz responded almost immediately, "Leah, when 'generalized' to the local population's language, often turned into 'Ludmila,' of which there are two short names: Luda and … Mila."

Bull's-eye.

Mila. Now, look below at the spelling of "Millenson" on Baruch's gravestone. (The Yiddish uses Hebrew letters, but it's not how the name would be spelled in modern Hebrew.) The name is the Yiddish spelling of "Mila." Then, note the "ayin," which represents the letter "e", followed by the letter "nun" to anchor it adjectively and then "zoyn" (or perhaps "zahn" if I'm reading a faded letter wrong) for "son."

Mila's son = Milenzoyn = Millenson

מילענזאהין

The name works for the secular authorities, turning Baruch into an only son, and it works Jewishly, too. Baruch's Hebrew (Jewish) name was Baruch son of Reb Nachum, the first name of his father. In the Jewish prayer for healing of the sick, however, we refer to individuals as the son/daughter of their mother (indicating God's attribute of mercy) rather than of the father (the attribute of justice). Baruch, son of Leah, in Hebrew and Baruch, son of Mila, in Lithuanian—or Millenson. A name both his parents could agree on and which was easy to remember!

This etymology may also explain why the name's origins were forgotten. To Baruch's sons, it was obvious that their father had been given the secular name of their grandmother as his new, draft-dodging last name. Indeed, this matronymic renaming was not an uncommon stratagem among Russian Jews. Either no explanation by Baruch's sons to their children was deemed necessary, or given the hardships of that era, genealogical history lessons didn't seem very important.

Interestingly, when Louis writes the name in Yiddish in his 1901 *Tageblatt* letter, he's already changed the spelling to more closely resemble the American pronunciation, "Millenson", (מילענסאן) rather than the Eastern European "Milenzoyn". Baruch retains the older spelling in signing his name in a 1906 lawsuit settlement.

While there's no way to be completely certain, the evidence strongly suggests that the Millenson name mystery has been solved.

APPENDIX B

THE "NEVER-WERE" MILLENSONS, THE "ALMOST" MILLENSONS, AND OTHER GENEALOGICAL HAZARDS

Sometime around 1850, Baruch Abramson became Baruch Millenson. Although this made-up surname would appear to ensure that anyone bearing it is a relative, the reality is not that simple.

The first problem is what I'll call the "Never-Were" Millensons. These are the individuals who alluring internet search results seem to uncover living in centuries past in locations as disparate as Kentucky, Kansas, or Gold Rush-era California. My favorite example is William Millenson Clifton, buried at England's All Hallows London Wall on August 25, 1761.

Alas, these exciting findings are ruined by some inconvenient realities. First, Baruch was Lithuanian, not British. His family doesn't change the name to Millenson but to a Yiddish name more like "Milensohn." Only in America in the late 19th century does the name become Millenson. Any earlier Millensons aren't relatives, nor is anyone named Millen.

As for Zelman Melenzon of Grinkishok, a son of Berel born around 1825 (according to JewishGen), perhaps his name change inspired the Abramsons, but that's pure speculation.

In addition, computer-read images of documents said to contain the name Millenson often turn out to be a different name when hand-written records are closely examined. In cases where the name is really Millenson, some digging finds either a transcription error or a random coincidence.

There is some genealogical good news, however. The anodyne quality of "Millenson" means that the Real Millensons never perceived it as "too Jewish." As a result, it wasn't changed by immigrants attempting to assimilate, the post-World War II generation traumatized by the Holocaust, or more recently, non-Jewish Millensons.

One more entry in this category is an odd listing in the 1920 Census, where a "Nathan Millenson" instead of a "David Millenson" is shown as living in the Louis Millenson household in Baltimore. Unfortunately, census errors are not uncommon.

The next challenge is what I call the "Almost" Millensons. This is a particularly tricky category, since the Real Millensons' names display a wide range of spellings. The most egregious example is the way in which Dena Millenson's will calls her Annie Millison. She didn't physically write the document and may have been unable to read it in English; her signature is an "X" designated as her "mark."

It doesn't help, either, that Benjamin Milleson and Benjamin Millison are two different individuals, not different versions of Baruch (sometimes "Benjamin") Millenson.

What makes the Millison spelling mistake even more confusing is that another Lithuanian-Jewish family in the Washington-Baltimore area is actually named Millison. To avoid barking up the wrong family tree, don't confuse Irving Millison (rifle competition champion) with Irving Millenson (pharmacist and retailer). Or Lewis Millison and Lewis Millenson, Samuel Millison and Samuel Millenson, Mary Millenson and Mary Millison or Esther Millison and Esther Millenson. Also, don't mix up Ida Millison with Ada Millenson or Ann Millison with Anne Millenson.

One trick is that while the Millenson family may have its share of wise guys, only the Millisons have someone named Solomon, the father of Deborah Ann Millison (no relation to any of the various Deb Millensons).

But "Lewis Milenson" and "Louis Millensohn" in Baltimore are really "Louis Millenson," a "Real" Millenson, while Annie Milenson and Sarah Milenson of Nova Scotia are not.

Name changes related to marriage, divorce, and death present another obstacle complicated by duplicate names and variant spellings.

The "Anne" problem is a genealogical nightmare. Louis Millenson is married to Annie Millenson, is divorced from Annie Millenson, and is the son of Annie Millenson, as his first and second wives and his mother are all sometimes called, along with, depending upon which one is mentioned, Anne, Anna, Hannah, Dena, Deana and Edna.

After Esther Stein Millenson was divorced from Louis Millenson's son Matt, she remained Esther Millenson, and her son was Lester Millenson. But Lester Millenson was also the name of a son of Jacob Millenson, Matt's uncle. When Esther remarried, she and her son took the name of Greenfield, and one of the Lester Millensons disappeared from the records.

When Mary Millenson divorced Meyer Millenson's son Nathan, she was still known as Mary Millenson when Nathan's Uncle Louis also married a Mary. The divorced Mary Millenson later remarried and became Mary Mandel, and her son, Barry Lee Millenson, became Barry Lee Mandel.

Two more examples of identical names: Rebecca Millenson is the name of Jacob Millenson's wife and is also Rebecca and Jacob's niece, one of Meyer's daughters. Helen Millenson is the name of the wife of Meyer's nephew Joseph Millenson and is also the name of Meyer and Theresa's daughter born two years after Joseph and Helen Millenson are married. Also, the Hebrew name for Helen is "Chanah," which can be rendered in English as Hannah or Anna.

Meanwhile, Byron Millenson is both an Americanized name sometimes applied to Baruch Millenson and the given name of one of his grandsons, the child of Louis and Anna Bennett Millenson. In a 1929 directory, Byron is called Baron. As an adult he's commonly known as Bernie.

In the one person/multiple names category, it also helps to know that Max and Matt Millenson are the same person and that Irving Millenson is known as Babe.

One more wrinkle: stepchildren. The son by a previous marriage of Louis's wife, Mary Gardner Millenson, was named Paul Weiner (not Paul Gardner or Paul Deiner, as is sometimes erroneously listed). He was a teenager when his mother married Louis, and he kept his last name even though he lived in the Millenson house hold. However, although Mary was not Byron Millenson's biological mother, he was so young when his father remarried that, in Mary's newspaper obituary she's listed as his mother.

This array of problems will also challenge those struggling to sort out later generations of Millensons with the first names of Michael, Susan, Amy, Leslie, and Debra/Deborah, not to mention recurrences of Ann, Anna, and Mary.

Hyphenated and hybrid last names, as well as women retaining their maiden names after marriage, could also add genealogical wrinkles. For example, my sister is Janet Ann Millenson. (On her birth certificate it was "Anne," but the "e" was dropped.) However, her son was never David Millenson (the name of one of Louis and Mary's children), but always David Edelstein, the same last name as his father, Herb Edelstein.

Still, genealogically, David is definitely a "Real" Millenson!

APPENDIX C

THE ABRAMSON CONNECTION

The Millenson family tree seems straightforward. It begins with Baruch Abramson-turned-Millenson marrying Dena Millman (or whatever her maiden name was in Yiddish), and the couple producing the first Millenson children.

But Baruch and Dena weren't Adam and Eve, and the Millensons were just one branch of a larger Abramson family tree. Trying to untangle even the first few branches that touch the Millensons turns up some unexpected findings.

Until now, we knew of only one set of closely related Abramsons, those descended from Baruch's brother Tsvi Hirsch Abramson (or Abrahamson). Tsvi, also known as Harris (or Hersh or Hershel), came to America about the same time as Baruch and also settled in Baltimore.

However, Tsvi and Baruch seem to have had a younger sister named Hannah. The tie to the Millensons was discovered by one of Hannah's descendants, Marsha Steinberg, through genealogical research and DNA evidence confirmed by Rachel Eisenhauer.

In Lithuania, Hannah Abramson married a cousin named Julius, who changed his last name to "Cohen," possibly to conceal the cousinly relationship. The couple eventually immigrated to Boston, where Julius's siblings were living. Hannah died from consumption in 1904, four years before Baruch and six before Tsvi. Many years later, her granddaughter said she had no idea Hannah had brothers in America—just as Tsvi's and Baruch's descendants never heard any mention of a sister.

Tsvi's family branch also takes some interesting twists and turns. Tsvi and his wife, Rachael Altschul Abramson, brought five sons and three daughters to America, although his 1910 obituary in *The Sun* incorrectly lists four sons and one daughter. Two married daughters (Fannie and Katie) are not mentioned nor is Tsvi's son Nathan. Daughter Hannah Abramson Handen's last name is misspelled as "Henden."

Earlier in this book, we suggested that Jacob Millenson was likely "set up" with future wife Rebecca Rubin by an Abramson cousin. The next generation of Millensons and Abramsons was also frequently intertwined. For example, a brief article in the June 20, 1909, issue of the *Baltimore American* tells of a party given by Helen Handen (who would turn 18 the next month) in honor of "Dr. J. Rosenstein" of Jersey City, New Jersey. The article lists the attendees.

Image: Helen Handen Millenson and her cousin from Pittsburgh, Archie Joseph, in Washington's Rock Creek Park around 1918. Their mothers were Abramson sisters.

Source: Archie Joseph

Jacob Rosenstein was a first cousin of Helen's; his mother, Fannie Abramson Rosenstein, was a sister of Helen's mother, Hannah Abramson Handen. Another first cousin was Jack Joseph of West Virginia, whose mother was Katie Abramson Joseph. There may have been other cousins I couldn't identify, but the most important (to me) was Joseph Millenson, whom Helen will later marry. Joe's paternal grandfather, Baruch, and Helen's maternal grandfather, Tsvi, were brothers, making Joe and Helen second cousins.

Their only child, Roy, was my father, who throughout his life kept in touch with parts of the Abramson and Millenson families. Yet Hannah Abramson Cohen, it turns out, was not the only invisible relative.

My dad was always close to his Handen first cousins. The last surviving member of that group, Shyrlee Belle Handen Hurwitz, granddaughter of Hannah Abramson Handen, has long lived in the Virginia Beach area. My research uncovered other Virginia Beach-area natives who were Shyrlee Belle's second cousins; i.e., grandchildren of Nathan Abramson, one of Hannah Abramson Handen's brothers. Nathan established a store in the area around 1890, his son Abe continued to live in the area, and his brothers I. Victor, William, and Charles also lived locally for varying periods of time. Yet, although the Jewish community was not large, even the knowledge that the families were related vanished decades ago.

Family connections often fade as later generations lose touch with increasingly distant relatives with whom they don't seem to have much in common. Some individuals may also deliberately choose to keep a distance from family, while others just don't have the time or interest to make the effort to maintain ties. Moreover, personal contact is far from a panacea. The stress of adapting to life in a new country can snap the bonds connecting parent and child or siblings. (Might that explain some of the children's names absent from Tsvi's obituary notice?) Meanwhile, mundane issues that have always frayed relationships can include lifestyle or personality differences or friction over someone's choice of a spouse.

Unfortunately, we have almost no information on the family dynamics among the early Millensons and Abramsons and only patchy information about the different branches of the family tree since then. For now, the full extent of the Millenson-Abramson connection has yet to be explored.

Image: Hesse Handen and Joe Millenson, who was both Hesse's second cousin and brother-in-law, on the Chesapeake Bay in an undated photo circa 1945.

Source: Helen Handen Millenson

APPENDIX D

TIMELINE

* Uncertainty in dates

1800s

1838* Baruch Abramson, son of Nachum (Mones) and Leah Mendelson Abramson, is born in Grinkishok (Grinkiškis), Lithuania. His future wife, Dena (maiden name Americanized to "Millman"), is born around 1842.

1850* Baruch's last name is changed to Milenzahn, or "Son of Mila," based on the Lithuanian nickname for Leah, to make him appear to be an only son exempt from the czarist draft.

1862* Baruch and Dena marry. He works as a shochet (kosher butcher).

1864 Yitzchak Leib (Louis) is born to Baruch and Dena. (Exact birth date unknown.)

1866 Jacob is born to Baruch and Dena. (Exact birth date unknown.)

1869* Baruch and family likely leave Grinkishok due to famine, perhaps for East Prussia.

1877* Meyer is born to Baruch and Dena on April 4.

1881 "Baruch Milensohn" immigrates to America in October.

1882 "Dina Milson" and the couple's three sons immigrate to America in June.

1884 "Rabbi Millenson" (the form the family name eventually takes) officiates at a wedding in Harrisburg.

1885 First mention in a directory of "B. Millenson" in Baltimore.

1886 December fire in rented Baltimore house where Louis and Jacob are making cigars.

1887 In January, Louis marries Hannah (Anna) Sach in Baltimore. On October 26 Matthew (Max) is born.

1889 In January there's a fire in Jacob's clothing store in Eastville, Virginia, and he returns to Baltimore. On April 15, 1889, Louis and Hannah have another son, Joseph, also born in Baltimore, where Louis is a cigar maker.

1890 Jacob marries Rebecca Rubin in Chicago on February 16. On July 26 Louis and Hannah, living in Philadelphia, have another son, Samuel.

1891 George is born to Jacob and Rebecca on April 17. Louis and his family move to Chicago, where he and Jacob both work as cigar makers.

1894 Lester is born to Jacob and Rebecca on September 7.

1895 Meyer lives briefly in Chicago with both his brothers.

1896 Irving is born to Jacob and Rebecca on September 1.

1800s

1897 Baruch is quoted in a Baltimore newspaper in April as an "expert shochet" testifying in a lawsuit. Meyer moves to Denver at about this time due to respiratory issues.

1898 Louis and family return to Philadelphia. Jacob and family move to East New Market, Maryland, where he opens a dry goods store.

1899 Louis Paul Eisenhauer is born on December 1 in Baltimore to Mary Catherine and Stephen Eisenhauer. It will not be discovered that his real father was Louis Millenson until nearly 120 years later.

1901 Personal ad from Max, Joe, and Sam Millenson on July 12 in a national Yiddish newspaper says Louis abandoned his family in Philadelphia and asks him to come home. Louis replies that he's living in Chicago but didn't really abandon them. In Denver, Meyer is held up at gunpoint while collecting money for a grocery for which he is a driver.

1903 Baruch files a lawsuit after being brutally beaten by another man, Max Shapiro (Shapero).

1904 On March 27 Meyer marries Theresa Prussick, a divorcée, in Denver.

1905 Nathan is born to Meyer and Theresa on October 10.

1908 Baruch dies on October 14 in Baltimore. On October 27 Louis, who has moved to Denver, files for divorce from Hannah, who is in Philadelphia, in a Denver court. On October 30 Libby Leah is born to Meyer and Theresa.

1909 On June 15 Louis marries the widow Annie Bennett in a civil ceremony in Goodland, Kansas. She has four children from her previous marriage. They live in Denver.

1911 Beatrice is born to Meyer and Theresa on August 21. Byron is born to Louis and Annie on December 1.

1913 Helen is born to Meyer and Theresa on June 4.

1914 A fire ravages Jacob's store in East New Market. He rebuilds.

1915 Annie dies unexpectedly on April 11. Her four children are sent by train to New York to live with an aunt and uncle. Louis and Byron move to East New Market to live temporarily with Jacob. On October 23, by then living in Baltimore, Louis marries Mary Gardner, who has a 14-year-old son, Paul Weiner, from a previous marriage.

1917 David is born on March 30 to Louis and Mary and is sent away at a young age to Rosewood State Training School because of mental disabilities. Jacob sells his store and moves to Cumberland, Maryland, where his sons have their own retail businesses.

1918 Ada is born on November 24 to Louis and Mary, who now run a dry goods store in Baltimore. In Denver, Meyer is prospering with his Western Beef Company.

1920 Dena dies on July 13.

1921 Jacob's wife, Rebecca, dies on October 2.

1927 Meyer commits suicide on January 1.

1928 Jacob dies in Cumberland on June 8.

1949 Louis dies on March 2. His wife, Mary, dies November 13.

1960 Meyer's wife, Theresa, dies on June 4.

www.ingramcontent.com/pod-product-compliance
Ingram Content Group UK Ltd.
Pitfield, Milton Keynes, MK11 3LW, UK
UKHW062005290726
14090UKWH00022B/1406